Christ in the Fog

Christ in the Fog

Meditations of the Functional Hurting

MATT LEWELLYN

To my wife Rachel, whose unwavering

love, affirmation, and support have

brought healing to the souls of many.

Contents

PART I

1. Fog

Billowing and blowing, cold and dark: I awake to the fog. Wherever I look, nothing appears. I can't even see my hand in front of my face. Touch is my guide, as are my ears. Each step tentative – if I run, I will fall on unseen danger.

Where did the fog come from? It is like a dream – I don't know how I got into it. I try to trace back to see where it began, where the first mists blew in, but it seems to have pervaded even my memory.

The fog is the now, what I live in the present. It is like I have become aware of something that always was.

Many of us know the feeling. It is a feeling that we don't often choose to feel, one that we'd rather stay away – and the farther away it stays, the better. When it comes, we want it to end – but we aren't always aware that it is happening at all. We endure it for a while and attempt to hide it as best we can. This feeling disturbs us in the very core of our being – an existential consternation that haunts our experience.

The Fog. Do you feel it? Sometimes it is hard to tell, but for some of us, if we are still and silent long enough, it is there. Maybe it's the voice inside telling you that you aren't good enough. Or that you don't belong. Sometimes it's the sinking feeling in the stomach, when all around you is well and good.

The fog can look like many things for different people, but it is a common experience. Throughout the centuries, it has been described in varied words: pensive, anxious, somber, melancholy, depression. And as disturbing as it may be in terms of life, family, and relationships, this fog can be especially poignant in the spiritual realm. Piercing, even – not meaning so much the activities involved in following God, as much as the moment-to-moment experience of God in daily life.

Perhaps it is a wall you feel that keeps you from singing to God when everyone else in church can. Or have you ever heard someone say, "You're a godly person," only to feel guilt the rest of the day because you've obviously deceived that poor person? Or do you have a sense of darkness that's always there when you're trying to see God's light in the Bible and in prayer? Somewhere, we've found a feeling or experience that we just can't seem to get over – we may visualize it as a wall, or a wide river, or a heavy weight. Something is keeping us from the joy of being close to God, binding as a chain to hold us back from fuller life.

If you're not sure if you know what the fog is, allow me to share some of my experience. I have always struggled to relate. It can be hard to put it that way, but too true. I can be perceived, while socially awkward, as a caring person, and that I am. But underneath it, I have a persistent unease that invades the rest of my existence. Humor is one of my tools to dispel the thickness in the air, and I use it often because it works for a while.

I experience impostor syndrome in many roles that I fill, from work to the church. Over the years, I have consistently felt less-than, as though I deserve the mocking thoughts that I think those around me are too kind to voice. Or their anger, or their disapproval. If I could just disappear for a while and let everyone get on with their lives... While I am externally quite functional, I feel like I have to put many pieces together internally just to make it, and it's a lot of work!

There is a longing in my soul for belonging – something I have found in precious few places, yet I worry I will lose what little belonging I have. Some days, I am mentally fighting through the swirls of mist that cloud my thoughts and emotions, trying to keep things straight enough to make good decisions and get my work done. When I am tired, it all becomes just a little bit harder. When I get good things, I find myself waiting for the other shoe to drop.

Now, I was raised by godly parents, regularly attended church all my life, started following Jesus at a young age, and went to Christian college and seminary. For years, I have been involved in evangelism and discipleship to grow the church, and I have been involved in the standard education meant to teach theology and discipline. All that to say: I am supposed to know how to follow Jesus.

Here's the problem: I don't. I really have no idea. I have always felt a distance between myself and God. I know, I know – Jesus has brought us near to the Father. That is objective truth that we find in God's word, and I believe the Bible is true. But my experience is not living up to that, and that difference is what this story is about.

As I've gotten older, I've discovered that as much as I wanted some things to be real to me, and as much as I wanted to feel, I had to be honest that it was not so: I am missing joy and peace. What I had instead was the intense guilt I feel every time I try to read the Bible, the voice in my head that tells me to just stop every time I try to sing to the Lord, and the feeling that I am not and never will be good enough to enjoy Jesus. Don't get me wrong – I don't doubt that Jesus has saved me. But being saved by Jesus and relationally enjoying Jesus are two very different things, and it does most often feel like there is a wall or a darkness separating me from Him.

Someone, somewhere, told us that in Jesus we would find contentment and fulfillment – peace and joy. In the church, we'd have a family where we could belong, who would share our troubles and allow us to share theirs. I have no doubt that many people have found this in Christ and his church. But please hear me – some of us are out here, trusting Jesus with our eternal destinies, yet feeling like fish out of water in the church, during devotions, and everywhere else. We see the depth of our shame, anxiety, and disillusionment as something that cannot be turned off with the flip of a switch (as much as we would like to).

We have something so deeply set in our psyches, so etched onto our neural networks, that pretending it could all just get magically better would multiply our harm. When we wake up to the fog and become aware of its existential crisis, we have to begin to realize that there is something about ourselves that we can't fix. When we trust Jesus to save us from our sins, we also trust him to save us from sin itself and its effects in general – including this brokenness, this damaged creation that we are. But just like we still sin in many ways in this life, we can also have this fog around us, even spiritually, holding us back with its moist fingers.

So, we want to find solace in the church – the church is where we can find Jesus, right? His hands and feet on this earth? Church is meant to be a place where we can feel safe, accepted, and appreciated. It is where we should feel that we belong, that we have family *as it should have been*, celebrating each other as we celebrate Christ in our midst. It is where the risk of vulnerability should be rewarded, so we can heal from our soul wounds.

Often, though, we find the church has its own business to go about – the practicality of Sunday school programs, sermon series, outreach ministries, Bible studies, etc. all focused on teaching people facts about God. We see the same tendencies in higher church politics, whether conventions, a diocese, or seminaries: the expediency involved in trying to get a massive number of people moving in the same direction in an efficient manner, and the protection of the brand.

And just like there was no room at the inn for Mary and Joseph and their needs, there doesn't seem to be much room in church for people like you and me to have our problems, questions, and concerns. Just as in many other clubs, everyone is fine or readily on the mend, so it can be hard to find soul care even in the church.

What began as a headlong run toward Jesus became a stumbling walk as we grew less familiar with what we're seeing. Starting to follow Jesus, for many of us, felt like a revelation of how we would conquer this life's ills. We learn to stay away from the "simple" sins, to spend some time reading the Bible and getting familiar with its contents. But if you go to church regularly for a long period of time, you likely feel the building pressure of the words and rules that make you feel less-than.

It can be the Calvinists who say that if you aren't seeing more and more fruit in your life, you're not really saved. That kind of message would work, if I was the least bit inclined to give myself the benefit of the doubt – but that has always been far from my nature. Or it can be the fundamentalists who line up more rules to follow, to show that you are one of the flock. They line us up and urge us onward in the marathon, when we've really been having trouble getting to the starting gate to begin with. It can even be as simple as the pastor reading Paul's urge to rejoice in the Lord – you're not feeling that joyful just now (or this year), so now it feels like you're living in sin with seemingly no way to dig yourself out.

Many of us who feel this way are the "Functional Hurting." We are at one margin of society and one of the least likely to get help, because to all appearances, we are functional. We can get through the day, at least most of the time, without emotional aids. We do our jobs. We pay our bills. We attend church. We spend time with our families. We may not even need medication for our slight yet chronic anxiety or depression – that constant, low-level hum in our minds that tells us things are not as they ought to be.

We are among the least likely to go out of our way to find help, because we feel most of the time that we don't need it, or someone else needs it much more, or we are just constrained by time and finances. Very few people seem to have the awareness to see our struggle, so no one is volunteering to give us aid. Practically speaking, the risk of revealing our true state is just so much greater than the potential reward.

This particular sense of inner chaos is incredibly persistent for anyone who has experienced it, but many of us haven't heard about this darkness in the church. There are good authors who have articulated its existence in various ways – but the dearth of first-hand Christian accounts and discussion shows us that a major focus currently in the church either silences this experience or presses people to rush out of it.

The lip service is that all are welcome, come as you are, and find acceptance in the body of Christ. But there is a pressure in the church that suppresses the fog: letting it out and discussing it might bring down those who are not yet openly struggling. And raising the questions may sow seeds of doubt for those of less mature faith. Whether that pressure is real or not, it is my perception, and so I do really feel that I have no voice to speak the story.

So here is the quandary we experience: I feel less-than – that is, less proficient, skilled, needed, valuable than the next person. In many spheres of life, I have learned to cope with this, but in the church, everything takes on much greater importance and focus. So, my first inclination is to be silent, since someone else can obviously speak better than I. But when the subject to be spoken about is that very experience of being less-than, my silence must break and be overcome – something that runs against everything I have trained myself to do in life.

In the movie *Fight Club*[1], Tyler Durden gives voice to the Functional Hurting and the multitudes who constantly feel less-than: "We are the all-singing, all-dancing crap of the world." Many of us resonate with that sentiment (though not with the way Tyler Durden would encourage acting upon it) because we feel as though we are running on a hamster wheel throughout life. We are all cogs in a giant machine, functioning in our responsibilities because we figure the machine has to work somehow. We do what little we can so that the sun can still rise and set on schedule, and then we can "get a life" to do what we love.

In the church, that means we are good-looking Christians, attending regularly and possibly serving and giving generously. We affirm the necessary tenets of the faith. We participate in various ministries. There is nothing we want more than for it all to feel real – but at some level that is not our experience. If all are cogs, we who are hurting are missing some teeth, and we have to do extra work to smooth things out for everyone else.

Our churches value our faithfulness and dedication, but most often they have no idea of our inner, hidden struggle. We are ashamed of our struggle. We would rather no one knew we had it at all (even ourselves), and perhaps that is why we are so devoted. But it's always right in front of us – when we pray, when we read the Bible for devotions, and when we go to church.

We can persist through it for a while, following the programs and patterns fed to us that seem to say that if we just hear enough sermons and pray enough prayers, we'll start to work through this stuff. But it proves not to be so, and we go many years without a real breakthrough in this journey – the sun is still hidden behind the wisps of fog, visibility is still impaired, and I have a brokenness that simply refuses to heal.

The fog dims our eyes to true light and is the experience of those of us who constantly feel "less than." On bad days, we know the fog as despairing that we will ever be better. In more high-functioning times, we see shapes and illusions and patterns in the clouds surrounding us that give us hope. New insights come to us where we find new ways to articulate our experience and have new words to speak to ourselves to try to talk us out of the crisis – perhaps even clear up the mists around us. But more often, these shapes swirl off into oblivion before we can grasp them, much less make them real.

Our awareness of the fog is fleeting – in fact, life is much easier when we forget it exists. There is only so much our awareness can stand before we can't take it anymore. Defensively, we may make ourselves very busy to distract from the experience and stay away from activities that promote our awareness. Unfortunately, that can mean lacking a devotional life, or avoiding prayer.

Sometimes it is our families or close friends who call us away from our task. If they don't "get" the fog, and if they are not particularly supportive in our journey, they may dismiss our quest as just so much navel-gazing. "There is so much to do for God," they say. "Just keep reading your Bible to know more about God and keep serving people to become more like Christ." Wouldn't it be awesome if life were that simple? And perhaps life is indeed that simple for them – so praise God!

Or sometimes, they perceive our struggle as a slight against them, or the church. That one can be harder to hear: "I guess you're saying that the way I've followed God all my life just isn't enough." Or, "You're being bitter, and you need to just get over it and get back with God's people." Or, "You're being selfish. Stop putting your own needs so far ahead of everyone else's."

Some people can snap out of unwanted emotions, simply calming down to stop feeling angry. They may simply flip a switch, "choose God" each day, and be all the better for it. But for the rest of us, the process is not jumping directly from "bad" experience to "good" experience but a long, slow journey to be walked. God is calling us to it; don't let your family and friends tear you away.

The journey leads down roads where we have to be honest enough to admit what we are experiencing. In other words, we need to give ourselves permission to be transparent, first towards ourselves, and then to others. When we do that, the process will lead us to places that really don't match what many of us have been taught as objective reality. At each point, we have a chance to re-evaluate: in some cases, our perception is amiss, but in others, we've been oversold.

As we walk through this book, we're going to give a voice to that part of ourselves that we are often encouraged (at least in the church) to cut off, silence and destroy. We need to normalize some facets of our experience that many of us think make us uniquely broken. We'll walk through some of the darker paths of soul-centered pain, addiction, and weakness of faith. Then, we can explore the ways our wounds affect the experience of relating with God and others. Finally, we'll take a breath, and we'll meditate on some passages of scripture to begin retraining how we approach the Word. Honest reactions will be key, as we learn to put shame in the proper place.

Of course, there is danger in going too deep, too fast down the rabbit hole. For many of us, though, we have simply grazed the surface – there is a danger, but it is far off in the distance. We often need to "sell" people on what we're doing, and that is difficult in this case because many people are defensive against an examination of the self. Perhaps they haven't begun their journey in awareness yet. Or, maybe they've been on one and didn't see it through, or simply forgotten what the journey was like.

In an age where any inkling of self-examination can be labeled morbid introspection, people are eager to show that they aren't anywhere near that danger zone. There is a status quo to be maintained, and the voices of the many pressure us to do so. For example, classically, men in America must hold certain "negative" emotions deep and unseen to be perceived by society as manly. This gives men the added pressure of upholding a prescribed gender identity and discourages them from expressing truth to avoid feeling less-than.

The problem with all of these voices is that they distract us from the real. We find ourselves filtering some of them out, because we cannot risk some of the possible outcomes of being more vulnerable. Instead of speaking or praying the first thing that comes to mind, we give ourselves a multiple-choice of some acceptable things to say, and pick the one that most closely approximates what we mean.

In the church, our age of positivism means we're encouraged to affirm particular statements over and over. Spending time considering what is true in our experience of God is discouraged.

We are driven so militantly to define our relationship with God in accepted terms that we lose the reality of our experience.

What does that leave us with? The sense that God isn't big enough to handle my reality.

2. Running

Throwing caution to the winds that have neglectfully left the fog in this place, I pick a direction and run. The fog is oppressive in its isolation; I cannot bear the thought of being within it for so long as it may take to lift. I feel it closing in around me, encasing me in a claustrophobic prison. So, I run, hoping to be running toward its edge rather than deeper into its depths.

In the dark and wet, I run into things I cannot see. I plunge my feet into mud on more than one occasion. Things like branches scrape by me on every side. I trip and fall, then get up dizzy and disoriented. But I have to get out, so I keep running. Am I going the same direction I started? Maybe I've gone in circles, following the shifting wisps.

We spend our lives moving around. We have big movements – picking up roots for a job across the country, choosing a university to attend, finding a spouse, or raising our children. Then there's the small movements – what should I wear, what movie to watch, how loud to have my music on, which fast food do I want today, and do I want the fancy donut or the one from the gas station (seriously, pick the gas station every time).

Now, these movements can be positive and life-building (even the small ones), and they often are for those who are firmly on the healthy/functional end of the spectrum. We could flit from one thing to another or make large jumps, and have at least a kernel of an idea of where we are headed and why. In the spiritual realm, we would select our church, our friends, and our close advisers so that we retain that vision – God is visible from his influence in our sphere and we are active in pursuing him with our lives and talents.

In the fog, though, we do not have that vision. As the Functional Hurting, we have our careers, our spouses, and our children, and we are sometimes quite capable of building our lives in those directions. Sometimes those spheres are more hidden from us. But especially when it comes to God and church, the fog swirls in and blurs our vision. For whatever reason (and we will explore some reasons in these chapters), we have a fundamental discomfort when we try to directly relate with God.

Since we are functional, we can make great strides even in the sphere of the church – learning a great deal, figuring out how that culture works, even teaching and leading. I have known good pastors who live with the fog. I've even known missionaries, who have traveled to the ends of the earth despite their fog-filled reality! Achievement in the church does not shield you from the fog, much less prove your advancement out of it.

Many great works have been written which further our understanding of Christ in his person, work, and lordship, but book learning in any volume cannot "substitute in" to solve relational brokenness. I've been to the seminary and spent my whole life in church – let me tell you, you cannot read your way into a great relationship with God.

We tend to stay quiet about our experience because there is shame in our existence. What we endure in our relational patterns from day to day seems like it should be simply our own burden to bear. We are told to encourage one another, after all, so we do not want to bring down any other Christians. For many of us, this hiddenness may have to do with losing face. But, I believe we also just don't want to be a bother to others.

We also don't want to give voice to the fact that our experience has these dimensions – it would be so much nicer if our friends' perception of our reality were correct. Or at least, what we think their perception is – that the person who is functional on the surface must also be put together within. We make that assumption about others, so it makes sense that we would project that on those who perceive us.

As much as we hold tightly to the truth that Jesus must save us and has saved us (for we have no other hope), our feelings (subjective experience) don't match up. So, we experience self-condemnation over that (as "sinful" as that in itself may be). But it's not something that can get turned on and off like a light bulb. The switch is broken, or the bulb is burnt out – either way, we are in this without a light on, and that naturally makes us uncomfortable.

For most of us, when we sense something uncomfortable in our souls, that little prick that tells us that things are not so well as we would like, we start glancing around like threatened animals. Our awareness has been drifting around the various parts of our souls and has rested at last upon a sore spot. A wound. A tear in our soul-fabric. We quickly take stock of the situation, decide on a course of action that will make us feel better, and get on with it, *post haste*.

In much of life, with normal everyday needs, it really works quite well. When I'm hungry, I eat; when tired, I sleep. But beyond some of those basic necessities of life, we start pulling out all kinds of ways to switch off that little feeling that it's not all right. When we get into existential crises, we turn to a myriad of saviors for a little rest, and each one of us has our particular few that we call our favorites.

Each one of those options has a place on the spectrum where we've decided it is "very unhealthy," "less unhealthy," "pretty harmless," etc. As Christians, we can generally agree on things like illicit drugs, extramarital sex, pornography, and drunkenness – those would be examples of the very unhealthy ways of dealing with life's twists and turns. The more occasional drinking to alter one's mood can be a bit contentious in some churches. But if we are honest, we alter our moods in many different ways (caffeine, music, binge-watching TV and movies).

Awareness is a blessing and a curse: we can see that we're reacting to pain and trying to get away from it, but the pain itself is a terrible experience. That pain affects us deeply, and we react to it before we know where it comes from. We started running long, long before our eyes opened to see the fog around us. The fog pervaded every corner of our lives, because the fog was blurring out the most important relationship we can have – that with the Creator.

We opened our eyes and now see the fog, and now all of the places we have been running seem... different. Now I sense that there is something amiss in each activity – I feel that little prick in the soul, and I intuit that those activities are keeping me from something more important. Now we are in an existential crisis of the soul: my soul seems to know what kind of relationship with God would be really good to have, but I am not there and have no idea how to get there. In fact, I perceive that there is something fundamentally broken with my ability to relate at all, let alone with that Most Important One.

And there it is, the madness that begins in the fog – my deepest desire is to relate with the One who made me, but my relational capacity is broken. I have a lot of coping mechanisms that help with that brokenness when it comes to people, mostly because I can relate with people when I want to – and in large part on my terms. With God, though, everything is on his terms, and there is no mask that will shield me from his gaze.

What do you do when you've been taught that the way to approach God is through his Word and through silence and solitude, but those places are where this existential crisis feels most acidic? So, I run. I find numerous ways to distract myself from that deep, inner disconnect that threatens to rise to the surface. In fact, it seems like I run as if my life depended on it – give me anything, anything but sitting alone in a room where I have no experience but of my own brokenness.

In my own life, I have been down many paths while running around this fog. Some were meant to be more constructive, and I may yet see fruit from them in spite of what brought me there. An old professor of mine told me that my tendency was to seek knowledge and wisdom as the way to climb out of whatever pit I was in at that time, and I believe he was right – I am one of those that psychologists refer to as "insight-oriented."

For a long time, I also tried intense ministry in evangelism and discipleship. While both are worthy activities, I have had time since then to look back on my motives for a lot of that activity and see that I was indeed running from my inner darkness. I have had isolation as well as hidden sins, and at times I attempted to face it head-on and stay in the Word and in prayer until that deep feeling of brokenness would pass (it never did).

The thing is, it often seems like life is a zero-sum game. For instance, any time I spend working is time I cannot spend with my wife, and any time spent with hobbies is time robbed from Jesus. And if I don't learn the maximum amount from an experience, I can never get that back. For the fog, any time I spend here seems wasted – I will never get that time back as happier experiences. I have one life to live here on this earth, and I am wandering through it in a way that seems undignified for what it is. So, I run – I must get things in order so I can get on with life as it should be.

But so many parts of my life are out of my control. I want to get out of the fog, but things keep happening around me that drive me deeper into its depths. For example, parents fight, siblings squabble, friends fall out, and the relational turmoil of all of those brings tremors into my soul. Stable jobs begin to shift. Family moves away or passes on. Slowly (or quickly at times) the list of things I thought I could count on to stay in place, gets shorter.

These are things that were helping me be functional – I may have a lot of anxiety, but at least I have this job to pay the bills and give me a consistent structure of how I spend 40 hours of my week. I may have misgivings about so many things, but at least my parents are living in harmony as life-anchors for my experience. But, out of my control, so many things that made me Functional Hurting instead of just Hurting are stripped away, and I'm left with the fog by itself.

Healthy personal boundaries would certainly help, but without those, I feel so much that is not even mine to feel, and I cannot turn that off. Or, if I have some of those things left that helped me be functional, I begin to wonder when they will get stripped away too – maybe the dark future I fear is not so far away, after all. If I have something built up around me that seems somewhat lasting, am I just treading water until the eddy sucks me under again? So, I grab my function-producing lifelines and run through the fog.

"Stop trusting in yourself," you say. "Your faith needs to be in God to sustain you – you can't keep all of those plates spinning!" I wish it were that simple. If it were, I would stop running, wouldn't I? But this is anxiety. This is a fear-based existence, and it often cannot be turned off so immediately.

So many sermons, Bible studies, and accountability groups stop right there, though, don't they? "After all," they say, "Jesus said, 'do not worry about your life,' so to apply that we need to say no to our anxious thoughts." So that's the application piece: we need to just turn it the hell off already, so we can start thinking/feeling/ functioning like we're supposed to.

But my fear is partly based on what I have seen in the lives of people who have trusted God. A lot of them have suffered mightily – not glorious suffering of persecution, but life just falling apart and massively sucking. And having experienced a more constant existential pain throughout life, of course I am likely to assume that I will experience more of the same!

"Worship kills worry. Every time." I saw this posted a few times on social media by a pastor. By any measure I can see, he's a good pastor. I went to school with him, and I believe he is following Jesus to the best of his ability. But words like this can tear a soul apart. If this connection between worship and worry has been your experience, praise God! But do not think it works that way for everyone.

The fact is, we who are in the fog have spent a lot of time in worship, and we still worry. In fact, we worry about our worship! If this little platitude were true, we in the fog, of all people, would have greatest despair, because it means, so simply, that our worship is so deficient that it can't do what worship is supposed to do. It means we really are less-than, that we are second-class citizens in the kingdom of Jesus, and that we are consigned to a fog-based life due to our inability to make our worry-engine quit sputtering. And so, we run, as fast as we can.

Running is exhausting, clearly, when you are what you are trying to get away from. Throughout your time in the fog, you may have different levels of health – the experience will vary over time. Sometimes, you may have enough in the tank to settle down and sleep soundly at night. Other times, the thoughts continue to race, and sleep comes only when you are completely exhausted. The experience of consistently feeling less-than is that of continually running from yourself. You do not trust yourself to make good decisions. At times, you may doubt your sanity.

When you couple this kind of brokenness with a harder-line brand of Calvinism or similar, you end up continually questioning your salvation: how can I think I have any fruit of salvation when I have this fundamental brokenness within me? It is easy, so very easy, to go down a dark, dark spiritual path, where almost every act, no matter how pious, is evidence that you have not truly been saved.

The worst of it comes when we see people, who have followed God for decades, suddenly and tragically leave the church. If they looked at themselves during those years of "acting Christian" and determined they must be saved, yet fell away, how can I take solace in any perceived fruit that I have? That circle right there is a spiritual hamster wheel – even in the fog it is easy to see that it leads nowhere. But if you hop on for just a while, you can be exhausted for years to come.

Once in a while, you will stop, look in the mirror, and start trying to fix things. Insight-oriented people will do this quite a bit – we know we need to slow down. We'll slow down long enough to focus in on a particular weakness of ours, or a new insight we've picked up lately that we think will get us over this hump. A few minutes here and there, though, and it is back to running the rat race again.

Where does it all end? Anxiety is a huge part of the fog – whether that's a panic-attack variety, or a chronic low-level misgiving that haunts everything. Things that could cause joy are questioned incessantly. Faults and regrets get amplified. We hold our silence, hoping the moment will pass, hoping we can stop racing. Eventually, the dam breaks, and our consciousness is flooded with awareness that we are truly broken.

We reach exhaustion, and we can run no more. We are still with ourselves, and the sorrow can be overwhelming.

3. Sound

For a long time, I hear a constant, pervasive noise – like gusts of wind going through rocks, valleys, and caverns. After a while, I comprehend some of the sound. The wind that I thought blew the fog in and around me, I begin to hear more clearly as simply the chorus of broken spirits, whispering all at once with the strength they have left. The thousands, and millions, of them all together dulled into rising and falling gales. I open my mouth to speak, but all I can muster is a hoarse whisper.

Each day of my life, I hear and experience many voices. Everyone does – there is nothing abnormal about it. We are designed for relationships, and so we naturally interact through voice. And there are so, so many voices! From our parents, friends, and teachers, to coworkers, and even the critical voice inside our heads. Each voice is telling us something about us, something about them, or something about the world around us. Some of it is true, some is false, some helpful, some harmful.

We get myriad messages from the entertainment we watch. These days, we also get a lot of messages from social media. Each voice can be felt as a distinct pressure on our souls – one that is pressing us to feel something, to do, to think, to judge. And, of course, those pressures are not aligned – we get them from all directions, and they do not agree with each other.

Our natural, normal development is supposed to include a keen sense of boundaries around us: boundaries that voices must travel to and negotiate before we pay them heed and allow them to shape and mold who we are becoming. By adulthood, we should be able to evaluate voices in turn, and have enough personal agency to decide whether we will allow the voice to affect us in some way.

When our sense of boundaries lies undeveloped, though, the voices pour in like gushing water and wind around us, driving us about as we try to listen to all of them at once. How hard it can be, to take a moment to listen to a single voice! And sometimes, when we do, that voice gets personal and cuts us with a knife, sending shock waves through our souls that reverberate for years to come.

If we don't have those strong boundaries, we're susceptible to being told how to feel, how to react, and how we must silence unwelcome attitudes. We are ill-equipped to ward off those darts – the ones that tell us we are weak, or that our ideas are not worth hearing, or that our struggles should magically go away. When the current of our souls has been flowing in that negative direction, hasty or even benign words from close friends can sweep us further down the river.

I find that some of those words become pillars in my own story – I've internalized them to the point that I see their effects almost daily in relationships. Again, this is the experience of the Functional Hurting – we can carry on our careers and fulfill our responsibilities, but what little we had going for us in the relational department has been torn apart and left us broken.

I hear the voices of those who have become the erudite scholars on many subjects. I hear those who have considered the many facets of life and have gained wisdom for their effort. Then, there are the voices of the joyful, coming together in harmonies that seem so far from me. Closer to me, in the fog, are the voices of the sad, the oppressed, the broken, the wounded – those for whom life is not going as advertised.

I try to make my way toward some of the voices that sound most confident and clear. Here, I think, are the ones who seem to know God and know how to relate with him – surely, they can lead me through this damp darkness! Do they not follow God daily themselves? They will show me the way – they have the understanding and truth to get me out of here. They will show me what it feels like to be valued, to not have to feel less-than all of the time. So, I follow them – yet from afar because I cannot think they would want someone like me in their presence, as they seemed closer to God.

Fog fools you. In it, you see shapes of things that look like promising exits, or places to rest safely for a while on the journey. On occasion, they are true sights. But often, the fog swirls a just little more, and the shapes are gone. I have traveled far in the fog to follow something or someone I thought I saw, only for that promise to disappear in an instant. It is a very cruel experience each time, as it often rips out a pillar of what little faith I seem to carry with me. I have had many of these times, but I will share one story as it is one of the closest to my heart and a wound that I have.

I had a wonderful pastor who seemed to understand following Jesus more than almost everyone else I had ever met. His reputation preceded him as the visionary who led a small gathering to become a mighty church, yet never pointed to himself. He is the one who preached to me in very formative years of my life, who spun many illustrations meant to jar the soul from its slumber. He talked to me personally about my journey to the seminary, and he was one of relatively few to speak to me in a way that made me feel valued and understood. He was a pastor over thousands, but he remembered my name when he saw me, even when I had been months away to school at a time.

One day, the news came to me that he had been removed from his ministry because he confessed a serious ongoing sin – one that he had been in since before I knew him. Just like that, the fog swirled viciously – the man I thought I knew to look for was now a weeping shell, confused and traveling through the fog. Just like me.

Some of you will read that paragraph and start jumping to

conclusions. Some will say he fell because his doctrine wasn't tight enough. Or that he did not cling well enough to the fundamentals of the faith. Or that his spiritual disciplines were lacking. We look for reasons for a fall – and in doing so, we miss the point every single time. The fact that we're talking about pastors should clue us in – if the way it all works happened to be that more devotion to the word and discipline would lead to better results, then you'd think pastors, of all people, would not sink into the fog.

And yet, we are so informed by our established paradigms and judgments that we will discard the experience of the most pitiful among us: a minister of grace who has experienced little but shame for a very long time. And for ourselves, we often try to convince ourselves that we know better. But we in the fog *do* know better, and so we feel and understand what we have lost.

Suddenly we realize the brutality of the fog. We thought we saw a light, and followed it, but it was snuffed out in front of us. We are once again fully disoriented. Worse, the tears of the leader we thought we could follow, now contribute to the fog itself and seem to increase its power. In those moments when the fog shifts and consumes a path we thought was a safe passageway, we start to wonder about and question every aspect of that path.

Something inherent in the experience of the fog is that the voices that resonate with us most deeply, may not in fact be speaking truth. I now realize that some of those voices may have led me astray in my search for clarity and light. If I have learned to repeat words and phrases I heard along my journey that way, I start questioning their truth – it all seemed good and wise at the time, but it turned out to be a rotten dead end.

Worse, I have been so shaped by following this path that I can hardly see the way back to a safer road. And even if I found what I think I'm looking for back there, was it really safer? Or did it just get me to this path where I followed a leader who disappeared? Can I continue speaking the words I learned, or should I ditch that knowledge and start over?

In the experience of the fog there are many losses. One of these is the loss of trust in voices around us. Another is the loss of our own voices. We awake in the fog, experience the disorientation of not seeing our way in a clear direction – and then we wonder what words we can bring when so many others are pouring out their souls already. I become silent because many of these other voices seem so much more eloquent, or loud, or likely to be heard. I will default to silence unless I believe that people (and God) want to and will hear me and listen. Silence is safe – few will disagree with it or press back. Those who do push, have often given up in the face of more silence.

It is as if the heaviness of the moist air in the fog sticks in my throat and drives away my voice – a laryngitis of the soul. Having no clear direction, my confidence is low and has not the strength to drive through that thickness. I manage only a whisper when what is inside me is crying out.

That whisper, it seems, most closely reflects my true self. The rest of me can be loud, but I know it is false. I can ward off the sadness and confusion with distractions and with humor – the louder the better. I try to show myself and everyone else that I am fine, and that I know how I'm proceeding in life.

All of those false voices will eventually fade away – as they should, since they are facades that keep me from thinking of myself as I should. But when most of them do fade, the one voice left in my head is that singular whisper. And lest you think that is a good thing, let me tell you, that whisper is the most devastating of all the voices. I am left with that innermost voice and no other message to counter it, and that whispering voice is my worst critic.

The critic speaks in my inner ear to tear apart my motives for every good thing I have ever done. It analyzes and re-analyzes all my words, searching for their truth and for why they are too careful. It is the voice that continually reminds me that the God-relationship I deeply desire is precisely what I do not have. It is the voice that reminds me of (seemingly) every sin I have ever committed.

Some would be quick to assign this voice to Satan himself, but I believe it is far more sinister: it is the neural pathways I have developed over many years of listening to voices like it, and so it has internalized and become far more nuanced and probing. It is the constant reminder in the fog that my greatest foe is not necessarily the prince of darkness when I have my own inner critic to contend with. But it so successfully dissects everything I do and think and say, that I have not the words to make it back down. Hence, I fall into silence.

My awareness of my silence presses on me most in two places. One is at church when everyone is singing – I often cannot bring myself to voice the words. So many songs are of joy and happiness – and that is so far from my experience! I cannot share whatever joy and happiness those around me are relating with, because I have never felt that God wants me to have that, for I am less-than. I am the sinner who always has many more sins to repent of before I can be happy.

In weeks when I have successfully distracted myself, that time of singing is when the fog comes flooding back. I long for the experience they sing about but wonder just when God will give it to me. If I try to sing words so that I fit in with the others, my voice becomes foreign, as if I'm an imposter standing in the midst of devout believers. (Seriously, who has impostor syndrome just for singing in church??) The sensation is strange – as if I hear myself, but I'm not the one singing. If I sing too loud, I will be discovered for the fraud that I am – silence is so much safer.

The other place the awareness is deep is in prayer. I talk to God because that's what God tells me to do. But I can lack the feeling that someone is listening at the other end. Or when I think about it

– someone is listening, but doesn't want to give me what I want. The reasons are many – I am not seeking him earnestly enough, or he wants to teach me to be less selfish, or I believe I must have some unconfessed sin (obsessive-compulsive spirituality), or my motives must be wrong in my prayer, and the list goes on and on.

The thought process of prayer becomes so nested and recursive that my voice in it becomes foreign, as if it's not coming out of me at all. My prayer is this object out there, outside of myself, which I've carefully crafted to somehow not offend God. It's a bit of a catch-22 where my words would offend God, but my silence would also do that because I'm supposed to pray. But it seems safer to be silent, because I might learn how to really pray later on.

What I remember is how often I have poured out my soul to God in prayer, because the words and feelings were exploding within me. I wanted to feel God's pleasure in response – but I didn't feel it. In those moments, it seemed like my voice had no power. I was laying it on the line, but not having the resulting experience it would take to keep me doing that consistently. If the Spirit prays with groaning deeper than words can express, and I pray in kind, then where is the close communion with God that should follow?

Through the movie *Chariots of Fire*[2], Olympic runner Eric Liddell made famous the words, "When I run, I feel His pleasure." If he can feel God's pleasure from simply running, why can I not feel that pleasure when trying to directly commune with Him? Instead, I am left with the voices in my head, the ones that put me down, criticize me, and break down the good I think I see.

I am now often thankful for music, because in its tones and harmonies and expression, music is able to express ideas that resonate deeply within my soul. In various forms, it provides a release from the tension, the anxiety, the rage, and the sadness that often pervades me. As I have continued on my journey, music is the primary outlet for that deep voice that escapes me when I attempt to speak. I wonder at times aloud to God, is that the plan you had for me? That of all my friends in youth as we shared the news of Christ with so many people, I would be the one to experience this deep fog? If so, why me and not one of the more mature of us?

I have more than once had my faith almost derailed in this journey in the fog, though I was perceived as a spiritual leader by some in college. Was I really – did I have something to say and to follow? Or (and here is the analysis of my inner critic, which has the uncanny ability to be cynical and right at the same time) was I simply making words that sounded as profound as possible, in order to be heard and valued by someone for once in my life?

And now, I have lost so much faith in my ability to say something profound, which was my reason to speak at all, that I have become mostly silent in things that matter the most.

4. Pain

The dampness I feel is the residue of the tears from all around me, the residual pain they ooze into the world. Do I want to see all those who weep around me? And what of those who yet see only the fog – who cannot feel or hear the pain of those around them... I see the dark figures dimly. What I feel with my hands seems to be a face. The face I feel is pitted, scarred, feels beaten.

Then I discover a source of the wetness – thicker than water, it is blood flowing free from wounds. I press a few places and pus of infection seeps out. Then I feel the pain, as though feeling these wounds and raw spots were feeling my own.

Is it my own face at first, or do I feel the wounds because I see wounds in others that I most deeply comprehend in myself? In truth, though I felt it was the wounds of others I touched to try to heal, it was only my own face all along.

Pain. Day after day, year after year, millions of people around our world experience chronic pain. Bad backs, worn knees, shoulders, necks, feet – you name a part of the body, and it can cause pain for a long, long time. We are used to people all around us talking about their aches and pains – we go to doctors, we take medications, we do physical therapy, we read up on pain management. We know that in this fallen world, our bodies break down. We accept that reality, and we have systems around us to help with it. And sometimes it isn't simple, when medical intervention doesn't always bring a good result.

Just about every one of us can think back to a time in our lives when we have felt pain. Some of us don't need to look very far. Think now, for a moment, back to one of the greatest pains of your life – were you completely rational? Was your behavior like what we want "good Christians" to be like? Were you rejoicing in the Lord?

And now, try to imagine having pain like that for a long period of time. A stab of pain may bring colorful language and the urge to punch a wall (and so add more pain). Chronic, unyielding pain is more likely to test the strongest faith, fatigue the body and soul, and leave the mind searching for some escape.

But here in the fog, we're not talking about physical pain, are we? The weird thing is, with physical pain, we're almost always aware that it's there. With the non-physical kind of pain, though, we often try to ignore it. With physical pain, people see the effects and understand where we're coming from, and often make allowances for us.

Non-physical pain? We have to hide that and try to hide its effects, lest we be judged for lacking a godly spirit or simply not fulfilling our role in the world. Or, we know and have experienced that allowing our soul's pain to show will make people uncomfortable around us. But just as we can't tell the one who feels chronic pain to stop feeling that and fix the wounds that caused it, we should not let people tell us to stop feeling our pains. Our bodies deeply bruise when beaten repeatedly – and the experiential blows that tear against our souls have a similar result.

All of us carry deep, inner pain. No matter how well we hide it in our daily lives, we have that pain deep within us, and it waits for our most honest moments to come out to play. In some ways, the longer we have carried it with us, and the better we have learned to cope with it and be somewhat functional, the more we can pretend we have left the pain behind. As convenient as that would be, often the wounds are left open, and we are still in the fog – we just closed our eyes for a while and tried to will it away.

We are the Functional Hurting. We are those who are trying our best to keep it together even though we are aware of deep wounding and pain. If the hurting overwhelms us, though, the functional part can seem to go away for a while.

We carry our garbage with us – it is, after all, part of our stories – and try to keep it contained in trash bags of many kinds. For some of us, one of the ways we try to deal with pain is by consciously categorizing our experiences in these trash bags. But for the rest of us, we pull bags off the roll almost subconsciously and just stuff things where they fit. Each bag is a coping mechanism – separation/ avoidance, confrontation, forward-thinking, self-talk, and spirituality, just to name a few.

We try to focus on the bags themselves and not the trash inside them. For a while, each one seems for a while to be the new, better way forward. But the fog has an eerie, peculiar power to make the bags turn transparent, and we can't help but see the trash within. It's weird, really – the fog obscures so many things we want to see and experience, but it brings such unnatural clarity to some of the crap we've long wanted to leave behind.

Emotional pain is hard to talk about – one of my coping mechanisms in the fog is to just not talk about the experience of pain, and instead try to objectify it for study. As if, in the effort to understand the mechanics of the pain itself and how I got there, I might see it as from a birds-eye view and find a way to resolve it. Or as if sometimes I feel outside myself, just seeing myself go through the motions of life while this existential pain seems to block me from being fully present.

But we feel it in the moment, don't we? And when we become aware of it pressuring our current experience, we have to look back to see where it is from. The thought of revisiting the past is scary, isn't it? And for good reason – we have wounds, after all. And once the floodgates are opened, and the voice is found, we could speak of our inner pain the rest of our lives.

For some of us, our entire childhood was wrought with conflict and anxiety. Toxic arguments between parents – the people who were supposed to show you what you are worth, tore each other to shreds. Wondering where the next meal was coming from – ripping away your experience of safety and security. Bullies at school – forcing you to grow up before your time. Lacking the skills that others seemed to value – and also knowing that if you had the skills, they would find something else wrong. The daily experience of feeling less-than – all of these are claws tearing against our souls.

Frequent experiences are the repeated blows – not body-blows, but soul-blows – that knocked us down when we were trying to gain footing in experiencing life. Some of this happened before we knew what existential pain was – and before we can remember. How were we to guard against the sources of pain at such an early age? It is truly remarkable that any of us is functional to the extent that we are!

When we were kids, we hadn't yet put up the boundaries that we need to protect us from the strong(er) people leveling attacks at us – the ones that want our time, our money, our bodies, and what emotional strength we have, all to prop up their own insecurities. We didn't know how to not feel responsible for someone else's feelings, because developmentally, we weren't able to see that only our own experience was our own. If we had that experience as children, where parents relied on us to feel good about themselves, that chronic experience picked at a spot on our souls and left a wound that is not easily healed. Some of our parents were not strong, stable people – as children, we wouldn't know what would set off the anger, or the depression, or the violence.

Perhaps if you look back at your childhood, and listen to your young self (because few others seemed to), you will hear yourself saying, "I'm scared." Or, "It was my fault." The tricky thing about looking back at that kind of experience is that our memories seem to trap us in what it was like at the time – as a child, not knowing that role-reversals were inappropriate, and not having any defense against them. Out of that experience, we come to consciousness in the fog, but it can be difficult to bring ourselves to a greater awareness – to comfort that child with the words we really needed to hear way back then.

And that's not even thinking of those who have had their boundaries violently broken – I cannot imagine that experience, but the effect on the soul is tremendous. One Bible story that has stuck with me for a long time is that of the first murder. What God says to Cain is incredible: "Your brother's blood cries out to me from the ground!"[3] Cain's violence tore a gaping wound not just in his brother Abel, but in the very fabric of creation itself. To be sure, all violent words and actions are talons that slice at sensitive souls, but it seems that greater violence yields an exponential increase in wounds.

Over recent years, I have read story after story of dear people who were born into and raised in the church, yet experienced the pain of violation in body and spirit at the hands of people in that very church! Many of those wounded souls were not afforded the opportunity to heal in a supportive community – instead, they were put down, disbelieved, silenced, and at times disowned. Their wounding did not stop at the experience of abuse – it continued for years afterward as the denial of healing led to festering wounds.

Leading up to the #metoo movement, many of these wounded found a collective voice together – and it was jarring for those hearing it for the first time. As enough voices rise out of the fog to finally be heard, of course they are colored by their wounds and experiences. I do not know why they were expected to speak with full objectivity, a lack of bitterness, or even-handedness. That requirement wouldn't be reasonable, but even when finally speaking up in an attempt to reach for justice, they continued to be wounded.

While many of us don't have those violent experiences, we do join those wounded souls in the fog – our spirituality and relationship aren't working the way they are supposed to either. Pain is a journey throughout life, developing as we grow up, grow old, and then pass on. When we were young, we had such high hopes of giving our best to God. We seemed to have such capacity then – so high a height to attain!

I can remember a time when I was a youth, and speakers would come in to chapel services and talk about "our generation" being a force – we were to take the world by the horns and set it right! But for those of us who consistently feel less-than, we have the experience of living in a land where everyone seems to have more faith than us – more experience of God. As for us, we're left in the fog, and it has become an integral part of our experience, extending its dampness to every area of our lives.

For a time, we think that being in the fog is a lack of feeling – we can even think of it as spiritual apathy. We feel guilt for not doing our best for Jesus. But we also feel an intense spiritual discomfort when we do get into the Word and into prayer time. No, the fog is not lack of feeling – it is what arises when I have allowed myself finally to feel, but don't have the integration of soul necessary to handle the sadness.

It is cognitive and emotive dissonance – we set our feelings filter to allow warm feelings toward God and others, as well as some joy. Then we read our Bibles and pray, and feel nothing, because the filter is wrong. Suddenly, the filter disintegrates and fails, and we are left with the real – which is what we decidedly do not want to feel. And then, we have the pain of isolation, because those other people out there are experiencing God the way they should.

The feeling of loneliness in church is a hard one to admit to ourselves. We try to find ways to explain it away – it is an oppressive feeling, due not just a little to the fact that the church is supposed to be our community. It's supposed to be the place where we feel safe, accepted, and built-up, "encouraged unto every good work."[4] Instead, we feel like we can't connect with people there, and so we try to figure out why.

My first stop, for many years, was to assume I was simply more spiritual than most people in the church – narrow is the road, and few are chosen, and all that. Convenient hypothesis, yes, but I was reading my Bible more and praying more, after all. No matter if I wasn't feeling the feelings just yet – sometime I will break through, just you see, and it will all be worth it.

Chalk it up to the arrogance of youth if you must, but that pride had a lethal combination with the fog I was in – my pain surfaced more by burning bridges than by crying out for help. I had to wander around the fog for a long, long time to figure out that those other people – they weren't the problem. And that, my friend, is a hard realization – I jumped off the high horse I was on, without realizing just how high up I had climbed.

A long fall down, and I landed at the bottom sometime while I was in seminary. Talk about spiritual disillusionment! Listen – if reading your Bible more and praying more was the path directly out of the fog, every single seminary student would be dancing a jig. Instead, a lot of spiritual battling happened inside of me.

The pain I carried with me was eating at my soul and driving me into deeper isolation. I felt like I could not speak in classes, even to ask questions, because out of all the people in the room, my faith was the least. I had to keep telling myself it would get better – it simply had to. It didn't.

So much exposure to facts and perspectives of objective truth, yet so little time to internalize any of it into subjective experience! That mode of existence leads to a dividing of the self in its own right – wounding the soul by clobbering the mind with facts and ideas while essentially stunting the development of experience.

Once awakened, that experience can lead to an intense cynicism: we were required to comprehend books and theories and come up with our own in assignment after assignment (and how little we understood! We knew not what we did!), but those running the school withheld (cruelly, it can seem) the key ingredient: time. It was as if they expected that such massive teaching in a short amount of time would be magically aided by the Holy Spirit. But in reality, they simply prevented the reflection and contemplation necessary for the growth of a relational spirit – where the Spirit would truly dwell.

What drags our experience even further down is that we often can't find a purpose for being in the fog. OK, we say, we have some understanding of the reason we're here – the cause of all of this. But why do we stay here so long and wander? What benefit does it bring to us, or to other people? After a while, it seems like it would be hard to let go of the fog, even with all the pain involved – it's given us some meaning and significance.

We somehow rationalize to ourselves that it must be for our betterment, or to in some way point other souls in the right direction. But really, it doesn't seem to be for betterment. All along, I tell God I don't need help, because deep down I think that if I need help, and if he was always willing to give it, then my time in the fog has been wasted. And how will we give anything to others out of a draining experience?

Those who know the fog know that they aren't talking about it or drawing attention to it. They would much rather it not be noticed, because light shining on this wound will burn their already-seared souls. Those of you readers who think you know the answers to these things: please hold your silence a bit longer. It is not easy to give voice to such doubts concerning the character of God. Of course, we know we don't understand. But there it is, isn't it – if we just don't understand, then what is the point of all this pain?

Trudging through the land of the fog is not a simple wandering. Those who are here know that awareness is fleeting – and that even when we can see a short distance ahead of us, taking steps in any direction in the fog is itself a painful experience. To move about in the fog, we have to be aware of the pain – and it hurts. It challenges our faith – why does God let us continue to experience the world, let alone Him, in this way? And our wounds challenge our grasp on reality: just as those who feel chronic pain may struggle to be fully "present", those who have experiential wounds and deep inner pain will show the signs of the same. Both the origins and the effects of the pain will intrude upon the consciousness, distracting from what is real in the Now, and dragging us off.

Occasionally, I experience a flashback to past moments of incompetence, insensitivity, general embarrassment, and so on. You know what I'm talking about from experience. This can happen when I'm alone. This can happen when I'm with other people. It can be remembering the opportunity I had waited for, then blew it. It can be the times I spoke harshly and out of turn – making and deepening the wounds of other people in my wake. Or times when I have been extremely selfish.

In those moments, I end up holding my head, experiencing the anxiety and shame again (or perhaps magnified, as that bit of memory breaks on me out of its greater context). These are the moments when I am driven to be alone, because it doesn't seem like I am worthy of being around other people. It occurs to me, though, that many things drive me to isolation, but my time in isolation is when I feel most worthless. There, these moments come back to me in greater number, because all I can see is that my time with other people was wasted, and I didn't prove any worth. Now, in isolation, I cannot.

Boundaries are so very important – my self-worth was always tied to performance, so in the absence of another person to evaluate my performance, I don't have that voice of intrinsic self-worth. In fact, the voices I heard in childhood, no matter how good my performance was, were usually along the lines of, "I don't believe you can handle this or do it right, so I'll tell you what to say and do." Or, "I can't believe you handled it this way! How horrible!" Which (understandably) drove me to isolation.

Pain naturally separates us from others and seeks to dissolve relationship. Relationships in the land of pain, on the other hand, stabilize our Present, but it takes a lot of mental energy from both sides – us and them. The distraction of pain drains us – we expend more energy than normal in trying to pay attention to what is around us, to people we love, and to experiences that should be joyful.

For those who connect to us in relationship, even if they are not aware of it, it drains more of their social energy as well, as they fight for our attention and Present awareness. Especially for those of us who are introverted, then, we relax a bit when the others go away and leave us alone – so we don't have to stay rigid and press outward to stabilize that Present around us.

If we grew up without healthy boundaries – being alone is the one place where boundaries seem to be less-needed, and there is some peace. But then, the shame of Past and the anxiety of Future bear in and collapse upon us – our voice is not strong enough to keep them off, and we don't have the relational quality to keep Present when we're alone. That takes a certain level of self-relation or God-relation, but our development there is stunted, so instead, we get the flashbacks and imaginings of things to come.

At some point, the distraction of mental and experiential pain reaches an extreme. Whether it happens when anxiety takes over our bodies with panic attacks, when general sadness blows up into depression, or when our own sins end up controlling us in addictions – those wounds and pains cloud what we can see in reality. Where we had high hopes for the Christian life, now we can no longer be so certain of our thoughts. If we fall into these states gradually, we become painfully aware that "taking every thought captive"[5] is not so simple as it seemed in our young Christian days! "Just submit every thought to God," they say, "and let Scripture advise."

In Philippians, the apostle Paul even lists out good things to think about,[6] that would likely lead to better-adjusted souls. But when the wounds and pains of our experience bear down upon us and cloud the present reality, they bring past and future with them into one murky cloud of fog: Fear! What if the eternal rewards I'm seeking are being lost? Anxiety! What if it's just my sinfulness blocking me, and I have made myself blind to it? What if these mental and spiritual troubles are all of my own devising?

What if, on the continuum of mental illness, from the perfectly healthy to the not-so-much, we in the fog are simply more nearly ill than healthy? What does that say about our ability to glorify God? And if we're being honest, that's not the first question in our minds. It's really: how long will it be before we lose the faculties we hold so dearly? We see people all around us who have lost their minds – we know they didn't choose it. In many cases, they were gifted individuals, contributing to society. What pain their loved ones go through – the spouses. The children. How many of us have experiences shaped by madmen? And how many experiences do we shape by our pain?

I am not so much the soldier, as I am the battleground. Will Jesus win?

5. Sirens

Wispy clouds form fingers in front of me. I barely see them at first, but I hear whispers speaking of deliverance. "Come with us for a while," they say, "then you may continue your journey! We take away some pain for a while. You can go on whenever you would like." I hear the words; my soul instinctively relaxes.

I listen to the voices again and again, and I am drawn in. The fingers start to wrap around my arms. When at last I draw back to leave, the wispy clouds become more solid ropes and chains, pulling me toward a deeper darkness.

In time, the clouds form a misty apparition speaking the words that I had heard before – but now also is speaking darker words of shame, guilt, denial, fear. Despite the airy appearance, the ghostly figure seems to have strength much greater than my own. I must get away!

As I begin to strain harder against the ropes and chains, and the hands that hold them, I begin to see searing burns on my flesh where the misty fingers had touched. Wounds are cut open as the chains break into them – old wounds set loose once more with renewed pain and infection, and new wounds cut fresh into flesh.

Everything in the fog becomes damper, heavier, and harder to carry along. Some of the trash bags where we carry our pain-garbage are better-equipped to hold what's inside them, but some are weak from being too thin a veneer, or too weak a substance. We're hardly aware of these things until they become a bigger problem. And sometimes, if the right trash pokes the bags in the same place for a long time, it breaks right on through.

Then the defenses are gone – more trash comes out. We try to stem the flow but lose our grip on our other bags, and... more trash everywhere. It happens fast, doesn't it? What was a concentrated area of pain in my life has just become a widespread cancer, eating away at the time I have to live in this world, the relationships I hold around me, and my very soul.

Let's get a little more real – and we have to, don't we? The world of the fog is one of a particular kind of pain, that we've talked about. But within the fog there is a danger to the journeying soul, a crisis waiting in the darkness, designed to entrap the weary.

In Greek myth, as sailors voyaged on a foggy sea, the sirens sang beautifully to lure them off course. These strange creatures lived on an island, and passing ships would be drawn onto the rocks. The singing was so irresistible that Ulysses had his men fill their ears with wax, so they would not be drawn aside or jump overboard. But he also had himself bound to the ship's mast, so he could hear the beautiful song without the danger.[7]

We who are in the fog are ripe for the picking in a world where so many voices promise peace (however brief that peace may be). These gods vow to give us pleasure, and oh, how down we have felt for so long! How anxious and in need of a distraction!

And after all, have we not suffered enough? Do we not deserve a respite? We are not the functional hurting who always think and act with majestic clarity. We are those who have experienced ongoing existential crisis, which presses itself upon our awareness and drags us down day after day.

So long it lasts, so much soul-ache, sometimes excruciating in the magnitude of our experience. Doesn't it make sense that we would try to take a wrong way out? Isn't it understandable that we would listen to the wrong voice, step out, and follow the wrong god for a while?

If we were thinking clearly, perhaps we'd consider the risk, abandon our course, and find a voice of strength to cling to. But we generally aren't thinking clearly, are we? The sirens call, they plead, they beckon. The voices fall on our souls like a drop of water on the tongue of one who has long traveled in the desert.

Our resistance wanes quickly – why not try this and see if it works? And once we head down that road... What was slightly fuzzy thinking at the beginning becomes more blurred, then twisted, then shattered. The disorder that follows makes changes to every part of our being – from reordering our neural networks to tearing fresh gashes in our souls.

In a world of addiction, I trust something to make my ongoing experience bearable. The first time, I considered it, knew it was wrong, but so craved relief anyway... I finally see a light at the end of the tunnel, something that will break the fog for a while. And the trust grows – if it can give relief for a while, I can do it again and again to have more relief.

We know what we're doing, most of the time – we can hold no excuses, even from our weakness. We know we aren't treating our bodies and minds as we should. But the next time, we just thought of the first time, how it felt good to have that respite from the general travails of fog life, and we didn't have so many qualms. Entering into each episode is easier – our minds and souls become sufficiently brainwashed.

I am training my mind by repetition to accept the break from the fog. I am training my body to crave it – the high, the oblivion, the orgasm – to the point that my physical being completely depends on it. So, I am caught in the web, and keep hungrily running down the path for more.

The run to addiction is downhill – and steep! The more I run down, the harder it is to climb out – and there are cliffs, too... Every time I fall in, I try to climb back up. Up and down, up and down – it takes a while, but I begin to realize every fall is a little deeper, and I'm not making it all the way back before falling again. And every time I fall further, I look up in shame. Every single time, afterward, I feel a more intense hatred for myself. Maybe not right away – the pleasure of the experience wards it off for a little while.

But make no mistake, for each moment of pleasure, there are hours of mourning. Why have I bound myself to this experience? Why do I let it consume my hours and days? Why do I let it isolate me? I don't want anyone to know what I am doing! After all, who do you trust with all of this? And the siren voices hold us in check, for it is much easier to continue the path of addiction than to either climb out or ask for help.

I go to church, and I don't dare speak – someone may figure it out. I keep a placid facade, lest I break down and confess, and let God's holy people know what a worm I have become. It is so much better that they do not know, or what kindness they have shown will evaporate faster than water on the surface of the sun. If they knew me as I know myself, they would surely throw me away and never speak to me again. And why shouldn't they – I am the thing that is wrong with the church, the hidden sin in their midst. I know what I deserve, but I dread it all the same, so I hold my silence. And I keep falling further, further down, and the fog gets darker, thicker, damper.

I thought I was getting relief from the fog, but what have I done? And now that small, bittering relief is the only one I can find, for I come to believe I have so offended God that he will not use me anymore. I don't lose my faith that he would save me from the very edge of Hell, but he will not want me among his people. Each fall adds to my self-hatred. Each fall makes my prayers more impassioned. Each stumble cuts the gash in my soul deeper, as I cry out.

Let's breath for a moment – this is heavy stuff. I can go deeper. I have been in that darkness – many of us have. And I never, ever want to be there again. If you've been there (or are there now) you may know what I'm talking about. The word "addiction" holds significance for a lot of us, and nothing exempts the Christian from experiencing its deadly pain. So, breathe for a minute.

What I have shared here describes an experience, but no words can do justice to so dreadful an existence. Know that you are not alone – other Christ-followers are going through the same thing right now. Writing it out is predictably painful, even reflecting on experience from long ago. But let me give you a glimmer of hope – there can be life after addiction.

Look – not a day goes by that I don't experience some of the effects of my experience. That's part of my story and always will be, but it's not the end of the story. I have regrets, and I sometimes weep at the memory of myself before traveling down that road, knowing the pain I was yet to suffer. But though there be residual pain and pangs, moments of confusion, and memories to be forgotten, Jesus CAN bring you through this.

There are so many causes for getting caught in a web where one action and one alone brings you some kind of temporary relief from all the pain that persists on your consciousness – genetic predisposition, prior trauma, bad choices, or maybe trusting the wrong person. And as you walk through the fog, the sirens sing and call for you to come, step away from seeing the darkness of the fog – just for a while, right?

To be in the fog is to be vulnerable. So many voices are around: some loud, others soft, many enticing. So many things, so much stuff out there to be found and enjoyed (or employed) for a moment – drugs, alcohol, pornography, food, television, cutting, on and on the list may go. We who know the fog, know that the line to cross into addiction is much blurrier than many would surmise.

Easy to get in, so hard to get out... From the outside, people are wondering, why can't he get his act together and take care of his family? Why does she keep feeding her addiction when it keeps hurting her? But from the inside, especially in the fog, we know that the behaviors can't just be turned on and off like a light.

No matter how much control we have over them, they contribute to the same sort of experience, where we have that constant wondering – "how long will I be in the clutches of this addiction? All of my actions, no matter what I'm trying to change, always seem to end up in this same place, where I feel good for a while, then hate myself again."

So, as we step through addictions in the fog, it's a new class of pain – not so much that something was done to you, or that you went through periods of time where your family/friend structures around you led to a fog-like way of thinking and being. In this pain, we're actually taking actions that contribute to greater pain. Even deeper, with every single action, we get to ask ourselves the question, "Is God still on my side? And even if he is still on my side, what if I do this again – will he be on my side then?"

"Just one more drink." "I know the picture is porn, but I'm just glancing out of curiosity." "I won't get addicted to this – I'm just trying it once." We get addicted to things because we perceive, whether consciously or not, some sort of lack – we're missing something in our lives. Relationships are not operating as God designed, and we can feel it. So we go looking for intimacy in a way that, to us, presents less risk than actually facing our issues.

Perhaps we were in the fog already, and the hopelessness therein drew us to an addictive behavior. Or, we didn't have experience with the fog before, but made some bad choices. Some of these things we do while knowing the potential fallout, but with many things in life, we act without that kind of forethought and have no idea what the consequences will be.

When we reach fresh levels of personal devastation – that's when we look up and think, how the hell did I get here? I was trying to follow God, to do my devotions, to stay right. But where those wispy fingers used to look inviting, now I see only this addiction apparition shouting my shame and guilt!

So easily I was drawn aside, and I feel like there is no way God can use me now – I feel like a complete failure. There is no joy even for the short while in my addiction anymore – even that has been ripped from my fingertips. Yet, I still end up walking down that road every day, sometimes more than once a day...

Devotional time spent in the Bible and in prayer becomes a last-gasp attempt to somehow break the cycle and find God again, an act of desperation. If I would only read one more thing or pray the right way, this experience would go away! A pressure-cooker – as if we'd not had enough trouble with devotional life already.

Addiction reaches down a road of hopelessness. In church every Sunday, we are encouraged to rejoice in the Lord, spend time in the Bible and in prayer, and not fall into sin. For the addict in the fog, those dominoes fall quickly – I know I can't have joy in the Lord and still do this stuff, but I am trapped in this black hole. Of course, I've tried to pray out of this! But every time I've done it again, I wonder, "Why didn't God answer my prayer? Does he hear me at all? Doesn't he want me to stop doing these things that keep me from enjoying him?"

Such questions! If we voice them, they get answered dismissively – of course he answers your prayer, but you have to take responsibility too. Or, God hears all of your prayer, and he wants you to stop. The people who answer us are only looking at the surface of the question – taking it for its own sake, as it were, and not probing into why we've asked.

From within, though, we see only the darkness – the first time we did it, we thought it was the only time. We did it again, but thought it would pass. A month or two into the addiction, we started to get scared... We stake our last remaining hope on thinking there is a path somewhere we can't see, a key to find that will unlock the chains.

When you're addicted to something and you're going through a daily process of falling to the addiction, the addiction itself is that apparition in the fog, the enemy from Psalms where they say, "Where is your God?"[8] And if we already had tended to a shame-based way of relating to God, an addiction will only make that worse.

For the Christian whose conscience is pricked by the actions they're taking, they know they're wrong, and at a certain level don't want to keep doing them. Every time they fall back into the addiction in that process, there's a severe shame involved. Shame drives us to hide, even from those who might understand. The risk involved in exposing our dark shame is much greater than the potential reward – people will reject me, and I don't deserve to get out of this anyway.

I get this message in my head – that maybe if I had reached out right away, I would have qualified for redemption. After all, it was more of a mistake at that point and not an addiction. But now I've done it for so long, so often... As always after doing the deed (getting drunk again, shooting up, looking at the pictures, etc.) I deeply desire for it to end, and I think, "That was the last time, I'm truly committed again. I just need one more chance to get my life in line!"

But day after day, we give ourselves the experience of shame and of questioning whether God would still be on our side. The longer the time, the more often the thought patterns have gone on. The more often those neurons come together in our brains, the harder it will be to break out of that thought pattern. Those thoughts become our new default – a template for how we've begun to perceive relationships and process everything else that happens in life.

We begin to tie in other thought patterns and events in our lives, and our reactions to even good things get bound up. "My job is hard and stressful to do when feeling hung over. I hate it!" "My friends are getting on my case about my drug use, but it's the only thing I do that makes me feel good. They don't want me to feel good!" "Reading the Bible and praying always makes me feel shameful and worthless now... When did that happen?"

We begin to question every single prior spiritual experience: Have I lost my salvation? Did I really have that experience of salvation to begin with? Did I really get a lot out of that particular sermon or Bible reading? Did I truly have any real kind of feelings in that time of prayer? Was I close to God for real, or just kidding myself?

Every time the addictive behavior is repeated, the questions are reinforced. After the first month, you think that was just a passing dark time in your life. After another month, you're not so sure... Slowly with some addictions, but quickly with others, it begins to shape our narrative, rewrite our stories, and consume every part of our lives. People no longer relate with just us, but also the addiction that has begun to define us.

Addictions are self-perpetuating – the shame they yield, and the spiritual confusion they bring upon us (we who were foolish enough to walk into them or were genetically predisposed to certain kinds of behavior/substances) makes it difficult to step out and reform the good habits that would return us to a healthier and godlier mode of life.

Even when the behavior has been resolved, at long last, those long-practiced, deepened thought patterns and relational structures live on. It's riding out a fierce storm on the vast ocean – no matter how we come to land, whether softly drifting to shore or dashed upon the rocks, our ship has been badly damaged, and we'll be taking a while to sort out the wreckage and start repairs. The shame that was there, and the thoughts of who God is and how my relationship to him works throughout all the behaviors associated with that addiction, the feeling that I am somehow lesser than another human being because I fell to an addiction, that I am broken beyond all repair, that even if Jesus saves me, he may yet not like me – all of those thoughts, feelings, and reactions remain and must be worked through over a much longer period of time.

Those wispy fingers that seemed so enticing and gave us momentary relief from other pains and confusions – they became those chains that ripped our flesh deeply, breaking the masts we needed to sail on, whipping us into submission. They wrapped around our arms and legs to hold us back. They wrapped around our spines to break us, so we could not walk away.

They poked into our relationships – especially those of family and close friends. They took away from the time to spend with our spouses, children, and friends. They diminished the attention we have to give. They reduce our capacity to contain the emotions and experience of another person (let alone your own, if you've been incapacitated by drugs and alcohol or consumed in your mind by pornographic images).

We can be left with a certain amount of cynicism – we know from experience how we hid the secret and shame of our addictions from others, so we know others are out there doing the same. It is easy to begin to regard other people, even those in power in the church (pastors, priests, bishops, cardinals, etc.) with that cynicism – I hid these things, so what about you?

So, lift your eyes for a moment and look around – take inventory, if you will, of all the things that are different now from what you thought and knew and felt and experienced before your addiction. The effects have reached far, far beyond our own personal little worlds.

If you are looking for others going through the fog, and you've been in an addiction, you may need to look no farther than your closest family and friends.

6. Light

Still wandering in wet mist, I come to a place that seems familiar and chance upon the blazing figure. How it is distinctly familiar in a land of similitude I cannot say, but it feels as if I'd been here in time gone by. The figure ablaze before me, the being of light, I see his light and feel his heat, but his features are blurred as like a searchlight in the fog.

With such dazzling splendor blinding me, I instinctively throw my hands to my face. At first, I hear a muffled voice, as though his sound were as overwhelming as the light. He beckons me in words I finally understand to draw my hands down from my face, so the light would touch and heal the wounds and flesh.

I refuse in silence, clutching my hands ever more tightly to my raw flesh. Shame! I am shamed and shameful, for I have dwelt in and been tainted by the fog. The figure continues to beckon, and I speak eloquent-sounding words of refusal.

He doesn't react to my words, just continues to motion his hand and speak his words of peace. I slowly begin to realize that my words are not out loud at all, but only within my mind.

I've known people who met Jesus, walked with him pretty closely for a while, and then walked away. Not just heard about him, not just tried Christianity on for size – they walked in step with Jesus as if he was their one hope of a better life. And a better life is what they wanted: the hard upbringings, the drug problems, the bad relationships had all taken their toll on fragile souls.

Who wouldn't wish these searchers a life full of hope in Jesus? Then one by one, from seemingly unrelated circumstances, each one of these people decided that Jesus was no longer going to be their primary focus. They'd turn toward being "non-religious" or "agnostic" – usually not outwardly antagonistic toward the faith, but not interested in being defined by it. I have known of others, less directly connected to me, who took up a more overt atheism.

In my youth, in the activities of evangelism I was doing, I once thought that if I just said the right words to people so that they'd understand, they'd see that all of their defense mechanisms would fail on judgement day, and they'd turn to Jesus and see that he is the only way of true life. I thought I could use my words to usher people into the presence of Jesus himself, to meet him so he would wake them up and bring them to saving faith.

I'd share with person after person, but I never saw the fruit of that work. Quite the opposite: sharing the word of truth so much brought me face to face with the reality of my own experience. Was I spending each day aware that my sins were taken care of and nothing separated me from God? No – each day, the gap between what I knew from the Bible and what my experience was in life grew larger, and it brought me to eye-level with the minuscule nature of my own faith.

See, so far, we've been talking a lot about our life experiences with family of origin, friends, social structures, and the church. We've looked at the fog, with the shame, anxiety, and guilt that it promotes, and the uncertainty we have as we wander on without a clear idea of where we're going and what life will be like when we get there. But a lot of us also carry this illusion that if we just really met Jesus face-to-face, this would all be different. How many of you have heard a message preached with something like, "no one meets Jesus and comes away the same?"

Yes, we can come face to face with Jesus in the fog, but let's understand something: seeing Jesus there doesn't make the fog go away. We come upon him as if wearing fogged-up glasses – his features are not so clear as we want them to be. We've searched in the fog so long and so hard, and we've put up with so much soul-centered distress, that it is incredibly frustrating to meet the giver of life in the middle of all this – and not be finally healed!

Among the things we've talked about in any of these meditations, this is one of the hardest truths to endure. Here, it's not just the platitudes of the church that don't measure up. It's not just the song lyrics that are diametrically opposed to our daily experience. It's not just the ministry programs, or pastors teaching in unhelpful ways. This time, it's not just the personalities of people in our local congregation. Now, we're talking about the Blazing Figure, Jesus himself. And now we have to deal with his words.

Cognitive dissonance. That is the best phrase I've ever heard to describe the mental experience of being in the fog, yet connecting with the Blazing Figure. We all know the words: "Come to me, all you who are weary and heavy-laden, and I will give you rest."[9] Bread of life.[10] Living water: "whoever drinks the water I give them will never thirst."[11] And on, and on, and on.

We know the words, so when we have lifted our eyes in the fog enough to see him, we know exactly who he is supposed to be. But we are tired, aren't we? So weak and tired, and our first inclination is to put our heads right back down into the foggy darkness once more. It is so familiar, and it feels like it is the place we belong more than any other place we've known. More than that – it feels like the fog is the place we deserve, for having so muddied the truth in our minds.

When we meet Jesus in the fog, especially when we've spent years or decades experiencing life as the Functional Hurting, it seems like it should be time for relief. Our souls reach out to this figure for catharsis – you know, the kind we see in so many movies. The protagonist has a *problem* and has to go through some *hard experience* in order to realize some *truth* about the problem. Near the end of the movie, there is usually a *penultimate crisis* leading to an *ultimate catharsis* that resolves the problem. And isn't that what we've been looking for?

We hang in there, day after day, functioning in our lives as best we can, holding on for dear life at times, so that we will finally get to that breakthrough moment. Distance runners know this as the wall: lactic acid builds up in the muscles, and the athlete needs to work through that to continue to the end of the run. Problem-solvers can experience this as well – being frustrated with a particular puzzle, about to give up on it, when suddenly a fresh, new perspective alights to bring a final solution.

We expect that experience when we finally meet Jesus, but in the moment, the events proceed quite differently. And so, we have emotive dissonance as well. On the one hand, we sense that we must respect Jesus for who he is, but at the same time, we are intensely frustrated with where we remain. There is no catharsis, so all the pent-up emotions we hoped to release come rushing forth in a much less helpful manner – we feel almost compelled to steel ourselves against the one being who would save us.

As we realize we will come away from this encounter still being in the fog, we get those emotions coming out that seem so out of place in church: anger, despair, bitterness, and, yes, hate. Please understand, we're not looking at this as sheep outside of the fold awaiting salvation from sin – we know we are undeserving and have no hope outside of Christ. But having eternal life in our grasp as sons and daughters of God, with Jesus as our brother, it seems so small a thing for God to release us from this experience in this life.

In truth, it feels like it is our fault – our path in the fog. We understand that in some sense we are powerless to change our experience, but we know his words! If we know the words, and we believe them, then we should be able to live them, right? And because we're not living them, and we *know* we're not living them (rest? what's that! never in the fog…), then we must be here by our own doing. We want to believe, and we want to live! But we believe we have all the life we deserve.

In fact, it's easy for us to believe that we ourselves are entirely the reason for remaining in the fog at this point. It's easy to believe that since we are less-than, there is additional experience Jesus wants us to have before we get released to that catharsis. Or, that we have to learn something more to fix our attitude for when we meet him in the fog again – something else we have to get right.

Let me reiterate – I'm not talking about getting saved here. That happened when we trusted Jesus for our eternal destinies, and I firmly believe that having placed our trust there ensures our final salvation. What we're talking about here is more present, more tangible, and ever-so-saturated with our current stories. When Jesus says we can have life, and have it in abundance,[12] how do I experience that in the now?

Of course, we want to have that present, every-day experience. But cognitive dissonance – what do I believe about my life right now? For the Functional Hurting, the constant drumbeat in our heads of negative self-talk and feeling less-than knocks us out of the running for that abundant life. Jesus says his words about who we are in him, but my thought-processes are so twisted around that I can't put that together with the man I see in the mirror.

It's not just habits, either – those of us who have been to the Bob Newhart school of counseling ("Just stop it!")[13] can tell anyone who will listen that this runs much deeper. No, the very wiring of our brains has been set for a very long time, so our bodies are fighting us at every step to stop us from thinking well of ourselves. When we do think positive thoughts about ourselves and talk ourselves up, it is usually in compensation for how we normally think and feel, and we are trying to block things out for a while.

So, what to do with the Blazing Figure? He says we can have abundant life, rest, and peace. I haven't experienced that – instead, my experience is so twisted that I see the giver of life and feel despair instead of hope. So, what happens when I do drop my hands, which have covered my shame, and let him see my true face? I expect a reprimand for not living life the way I should have – not believing his words enough to step into and experience their truth.

I expect that reprimand for being angry with him, for judging him against my very limited wisdom, for being bitter about the fog-life I seem marooned in. Of course, I feel that way – I recognize the Blazing Figure is God, and this is the God-image I have practiced for so long. The God who tires of our excuses and expects better. The God who simply pitied us enough to die for us. The God who ransomed a whole lot of fog-bound souls.

They say that Christianity is not about religion – it's a relationship. But it is really, really hard to have a one-sided experience of relationship. I read, and I pray, and I rarely, if ever, "hear God's voice." When I do, I always question the experience (because cessation of gifts, and all that, right?). After all, if I finally hear what I want to hear, am I just deluding myself, or did it really happen? And if I hear what I fear (and expect), then all is confirmed. And, if I hear what I do not expect, then what else am I wrong about – and what little solid ground I feel in the swampy fog begins to disintegrate.

So, when I finally embrace my condition in the fog enough to lift my head a little and see the Blazing Figure standing there, is it really so unnatural that I shrink back? Is it so strange that I don't know what to say? And is it so weird that I feel like I really don't know who he is and what he's about?

What is even harder is seeing from afar those Christians who seem to have this relationship thing down. They are all the more certain of God's voice in their lives. Sure, they have struggles, but not this existential stuff we've been talking about. And they certainly seem to feel peace regularly.

Remember the cool kids in school – the ones who seemed to be able to talk to anyone, easily make friends, and bring value to a room? I wasn't one of them – I was less-than, more or less second-class, and always fighting to prove my value in any circle of people. Here we are again – the "cool" Christians are able to talk to anyone. They can talk to God and hear his voice, and they can talk to other people about their joy in Him. They easily make friends – with God and with people.

I know God and I believe what he says about himself, but I have a hard time hearing his voice to me. I have a hard time talking to other people because I have this "value conversation" going on in my head all the time – is what I am saying or something about me valuable enough for this person to spend their time talking with me? Well, that valuation happens with God too, and it always seems like he has enough cool Christians to occupy him.

Look – this all sounds like I make excuses for the words of Jesus. In a sense, I am – I'll admit that I thought the words I heard should match my ongoing experience, but my experience is nothing like it. For my friends who have walked away from God in various ways and measures, I get it. The cognitive dissonance is unutterably hard to handle. I "know" so many things, but the "feeling" is so different.

"Ignore the feeling," some say, "and simply follow the Bible" – but I find their devotion a bit suspect. Should I not want my experience to match what I "know" to be true? And should I not be disturbed when it does not match up? Because it does not match, and I also have mismatched emotions in response, which tears at the fabric of the soul. According to what I've learned while being raised in the church, feeling this way means I have failed – that I am a failure.

When we have this level of dissonance going on for so long, it is natural to look for something to change to eliminate the distress. And if I have spent many years studying the Bible and allowing the truths there to inform my gut-level responses to this world and this life, and my gut tells me that the fog is all wrong, and life in Jesus should not be this way, then what? The fog is still my experience, so somehow the dissonance must reconcile.

See, we live in an age when atheists are many, and they are bold enough to describe the reasons they reject the idea of a God-defined reality. They give their many causes they would be sure to present to God (in their minds, of course, on the off-chance he does exist) as charges against his nature. What they describe are real problems, and I get it! It would be easier, wouldn't it, to not have the cognitive dissonance – to not have to hear the words again and again and again while knowing they don't describe our daily experience.

It would be easier, wouldn't it, to not have to explain suffering. Suffering bothers me greatly, especially the suffering of innocents. "Knowing" about original sin, or even total depravity, does not solve the emotion. For the losses some of my friends have experienced with their children, I wept and I cried out, not just in grief but in anger! I could not fathom how a good, merciful, and holy God would allow this to happen! I've had friends whose children were born with deformities or other disabilities, and I cannot fathom that either. And what of the many who die before they are born?

There is no knowing that can solve feeling. And there is no willpower that can solve feeling either. We are human beings made up of thoughts, emotions, and a will. We have to have all three working together – we cannot team up thought and will to make emotion be silent and go away.

The problem of God and evil is one of the big reasons people walk away from Jesus. And if you read the Bible, the problem doesn't begin and end with just the bad things that happen to people. We have hard, difficult truths in the Bible that are emotionally difficult to accept. In Joshua 7, for example, a man, Achan, brought God's anger on Israel, and so they lost a battle. And then Achan and his entire family were punished.

Aside from all the killing that goes on in the story, which is hard enough to handle, when I read Joshua 7, I see in my mind's eye a man having stones hurled at him. And when the people were done with him, they stoned each of his sons. And his daughters. What do you feel when you read of that kind of brutality? Would you be comfortable watching that video? I don't think we should be - but the speed at which many Bible lessons and sermons careen past these stories gives us pause.

There are many examples of this kind of violence throughout the Bible, and many of us in the fog are not satisfied with the answers we receive when we ask pointed questions about it. We cannot be, when we are given a simple moral lesson out of all of this violence, and we would ask more complex questions about what these stories tell us about God. And this blazing figure is the very same who commanded it all be done, and the very same who commanded we love our enemy.

Cognitive dissonance, and emotional dissonance - I get how someone comes to the conclusion that God may be bad or that God may not exist. We are told to have faith - something that we cannot seem to just conjure up for ourselves, and that faith which we do have is challenged by all of these things.

Another problem is the reality that a very large number of those who claim to follow Jesus, simply do not live their lives as he told them to. I have seen so many in this ongoing parade - let's start with the fallen pastors. Men and women who have gone through the training, the years of study, and the self-denial to become ministers, who then lose their entire life's work in inglorious fashion. Frankly, if the professionals can't handle it, how can we the people?

Or, how about the treatment of children who have been abused in church culture - whether physically, emotionally, or spiritually? There have been so many who were expected to repent for sins they did not commit, apologize to an abuser, accept gaslighting about their experiences, and continue to be denied justice for years and decades. Or, how about the times when the church should have been at the forefront of understanding truths concerning humanity, culture, and organizations, but missed the boat entirely (I'm looking at you, conversion therapy, and you, segregation)?

For those who walked away, at the very least, they were honest. They were aware of the cognitive dissonance, and tried to solve it. Honesty is good, of course, but it's just as honest to declare that I don't know. And given the experience of the fog, and the confusion of what I see, and realizing that my perception doesn't always match reality, it seems likely that I don't have the answers.

Some of us have tried this honesty in the church, and we have found out that the church is not a safe place for this type of vulnerability. That's when we get dismissed as second-class Christians, because we just don't seem to have enough faith to get past these "simple" questions. See, I understand – I wanted to rock this Christianity thing. I thought, hey, I was brought up right, I know how to act right, and I stayed engaged in the church when many young people were walking away from the faith of their parents. It seemed like it should work out that way, that my pedigree and willpower should make me more spiritual. But I've prayed and prayed and prayed for things, and so much of what I pray for just does not happen.

None of my upbringing, activities, dedications, and intentions have made my faith any greater. I am stuck in a fog that swirls around me, obscuring my vision, and the thing I want most is to see. I did so much activity in evangelism and in discipleship because I really, really wanted the world and God to work that way – that if I put in that much effort for ministry, I would see people come to Jesus – and I would have firm, concrete vision of God's work. But it wasn't happening.

One time I visited the seminary before attending as a student, and my perception was that I would essentially be alone in what I was experiencing, since everyone I met was seeing God work. And, I was just beginning to get a sense of how long the fog would continue.

I truly began wondering if God was really out there. I talked it through, so briefly, with a good friend when I got back, and his quick response was, "and I hope we've gotten past that." Well, no, my friend, I haven't – not then, and not now. In the church, all around us, are more souls quite like me. I am not so strong as I would have hoped. I am "ye of little faith".

Which cognitive dissonance am I willing to endure? The one where I'm asked to sing of an emotional state that is not true of my experience – to subscribe to a relatively recent tradition that Jesus will make me happy? Or, the one where I believe I am not deserving of God's favor but he gives it anyway? I am more comfortable with the latter. But I am still addicted to a particular way of being myself, so I guard my weakness.

Time and time again I come face to face with the Blazing Figure in the fog. Again, and again, I finally progress beyond all the mixed-up thoughts in my head, enough to hear his words again and experience the dissonance once more. He beckons me to give up and rest. I hear it clearly, for once, and consider it again. Then the shame of my experience floods in, and I whisper to the Blazing Figure, "No."

Then I put my head back down in the fog, and hope to "wake up" again to the sunlit life where I work, do life with my family, go to church, and explore any of the escapes I so neatly choose for myself. The retreat to within is hard-coded in my psyche. I tell myself the cognitive dissonance is too much. I tell myself I am not ready to experience that abundant life – I wouldn't know what to do with it if I had it each day.

I have so hard a time relating with people from day to day, that I wonder what having consistent relationship with God in a two-sided fashion would look like, anyway. And so, life goes on, and that close encounter with the Blazing Figure fades a bit. But the fog is ever real in my experience, and so I am drawn along its paths again and again. So, the Figure comes back to my consciousness, my mental conversations continue, and so goes the circle...

Some may walk away for good and use that as one of their escapes. For myself, I continue on this circular path – in the fog. At a certain level, I know I will be back. In truth, I am so stuck in my own little world, my faith so weak, my grasp of the blazing figure's character so futile, my hearing of his words so faint – I continue in self-preservation mode. Is it any wonder? Who have I met that can contain all I have become?

I have no analog for a Christ-ward relationship. But I have not walked away from Jesus for this reason: I do believe that Jesus cares about the dissonance of truth and experience as much and more than I do, and I believe it brings him pain as well.

And I believe that Jesus has experienced more of that dissonance than I ever will.

7. Separation

The words I speak aloud, finally, are that I don't need his help. At first in a hoarse whisper, but repeated – in time, louder than a yell. Expose my true face? This is sure to produce rejection! Maybe this figure of light will be nice to me, but he will only pity my wounds, not heal. I am fine, after all – I can cover these wounds which will eventually be numb anyway. Never mind that they fester, that they will harden in wood-like scabs in time.

I walk away, considering in detail how I will help myself – building skill, being empathetic, acting to help others, even promoting the worship of this being of light. The mists of the fog are swirling again, as clear sight of the blazing figure fades into memory, and I begin to feel around for paths I thought I knew.

Wait, what? Wasn't meeting the blazing figure supposed to be the start of a final journey out of the fog? "Oh surely," you say, "if I had been there, I would have stayed with him." Perhaps you would. Perhaps you're at that point in the journey, where you would stay with the Savior and allow him to bless you. Perhaps you are beyond the escapes or over your shame.

But friend, do not forget your time in the fog, and do not forget those who still wander in its enormous depths! Understand, we wanted to walk out of the fog with him and journey away to better things. We've begun to comprehend, though, that he wasn't going to immediately take us out of the fog or clear it up. Instead, he wanted us to stay with him in it.

In relationships, we all react to things differently – words that bring warmth and joy to one may certainly cause another to back away. The experience of the fog is one of twisted reactions. If we reacted to things the way we were supposed to, we wouldn't have been in this fog to begin with, would we?

But even for those of us still here, still in the mists, if we back up for a minute and consider what's going on, it can seem a bit confusing to us too. We've set out resolutely from the blazing figure, and what starts as a confident hike back into the cloud becomes a stumbling walk. Very soon, we start to wonder what in the world made us come back out here. Having set foot in the promised land of the presence of one who was at the same time blinding and welcoming, now we have neither light nor warmth.

Many of us have had a type of "mountaintop" spiritual experience – that big high feeling that tells us we are loved by a Savior and are part of a wonderful creation. Many come off that high (which is a good and valuable experience) and settle into a daily routine that's just a little closer to God than they were before. Good for them, I say, but remember we're talking about the Functional Hurting: what follows the mountaintop for them?

Well, for the hurting, often the journey up to and over the mountaintop is spent wondering, is this it? Is this as good as it gets? And all too soon the apex has passed, a blip on the radar with the knowledge in our bones that the path ahead is down, down, down.

We are left with regret that we didn't feel more when we had the chance. We are left with guilt that we made the experience less than it should have been – that we poured cold water on the fire of God. We are left with shame that there's something wrong with us – if we were right in spirit, the mountaintop would have been much more meaningful! We are left with fear – what if that was the last time, and it does not happen again?

As we descend, we begin to understand in our minds, or at least to rationalize – we didn't feel like we belonged up there, and so we came down by ourselves. We didn't feel like we belonged up there, so we didn't feel welcome to experience that high, that divine presence, as much as we might have.

Then we go to church the next week, and they're all singing, "My chains fell off, my heart was free."[14] They sing with heart, with conviction, and with joy – their underlying experience of God is flowing out. And we feel profound, deep sadness as we can't sing those words or echo the chorus of voices who can.

We know, if we ask the same old questions of why we feel this way, we're going to get the same old answers: we need to think about God and heaven more, read our Bibles more, pray more, and look for hidden sin and bad attitudes. Thanks, I'll get right on that. But those responses never resolved the deeper problems.

And so, the contrast: we stepped into the presence of the blazing figure – what should have been a mountaintop experience. Then we walked away because we didn't feel like we belonged there – like we would be accepted and blessed. We felt like this figure would (or should) really have nothing to do with us – we don't deserve his help, and we used the one way we had to control that. And where did we walk? Back into the fog, the same fog we've been trying to get away from, because we don't want to belong there either.

But if we're honest, there's something else going on. Our stories are not so simple as to just have ourselves, the fog, and the blazing figure. Perhaps we are the protagonist in our own tales, and the fog is the evil villain. But there are other actors in our stories, other characters who relate to us in many fashions and hold many roles. In any good story, all of the characters build and develop as they interact with each other and feed into one another through relationship.

And we acknowledge other people in life, whether that is our families, or our friends. Coworkers. Church mates. Surrounding actors – government, educators, janitors, fast food workers – all form part of our story in some way, and we are at least passingly aware of the relationship, however brief or fleeting or tangential it may be. But for those of us in the fog, there is one actor in our stories that seems to be more static: God himself. People in our lives talk to us, interact, spend time, speak kind words, get frustrated, and relate in all kinds of ways on all kinds of levels. With God, though, we seem a bit stuck.

It's all a bit tricky to describe, really. As I look through world history, I can see God as a moving picture, an active force and relator. I believe the Bible is true – God is described as one who intervened in all of human experience, and even became a human himself in Jesus. I see him active in my friends' lives. I also see how he has directed my life up to now in many ways. All of that is spread out for remembrance and study – observed like a painting on a canvas. But not experienced: I cannot get away from the daily, in-the-moment feeling of stillness.

You know those church services where in the middle of the prayer, the pastor says, "Now I want you to pray silently and ask God to speak to you." You've been there – what happens? For me, nothing. It's kind of the same as those other services where the pastor says, "Now I want you to spend a moment praying in silence to God to confess your sins." He wraps it up about 20 seconds later to continue the service, and I'm still wondering, where do I start? Maybe it is the mountain of brokenness that I see between myself and my God, but I can't seem to hear him.

When I went to college, a friend of mine gave me a Palm Pilot. Remember those? At the time, while not state of the art, it was a really nice way to take notes, keep track of a schedule, and just generally have my life organized. It was great, for a while, and then one day the screen cracked. All of a sudden, I couldn't use the screen anymore.

The crack made the screen unreadable – the colors would bleed all over the place within the screen, with just blobs of color all over. I couldn't just pull it out of my pocket and see what was next in my day, or refer back to some notes. As a little computer, it was still working behind the scenes, but I couldn't see it.

My experience of God is similar – I can't see the movement when I'm looking at it in the present. There's a cracked screen between us; the relationship apparatus is damaged. He's still working in the background, and that's great – but I'm missing out on a significant part of what life could be.

Life with a cracked screen is lived with a measure of confusion. The way I react to things won't make sense to people who have their screens intact. They have their mountaintop experiences and perceive that all is great and wonderful. In reaction, I say, "Yeah, that must have been something! But I didn't really get there." They're looking at a moving picture on their screens, and can sing of chains falling off.

I see a crack in a screen, a static picture that has blurs and blobs but nothing I can really make out in the present. So, it's easier to see God as a static force instead of a person – I see the effects rather than the cause. The crack in the screen obscures much of what many would call a relationship, and I'm left guessing at what he is doing and saying in the present, and guessing at what I should do next.

It's hard to build a godly life around a still image that stands in for a moving picture. There is great difficulty in relating when one does not know, fundamentally, how to relate. Some of us had intact screens for a while, and some experience cracked the screen and brought us into the fog. Others have had broken spiritual Palm Pilots for as long as we can remember.

Whatever the case, we either remember the clear screen or have some idea of what it would be like. Many of us still act like we can see it clearly and expect others to act accordingly. We know that those with clear screens go to church, they pray, they read their Bibles, and do all of those things that good Christians do. We also know that there's something wrong with us, and so our experience does not match up to theirs.

For some of us, that knowledge can come out as a judgmental attitude. If we're in the fog and can carry on a "functional" relationship with God and church (at least by logging the prescribed activities), what's with all of "those people" who do not do all of those "things" even though they have the better relational apparatus? I know many pastors here, many church leaders, and many friends who think this way – they wonder why people who can read are not reading their Bibles, why people who can speak are not praying, and why people who seem to have time for all else do not come to the activities of the church. I understand them, because I was one of them.

We all project the ideal we hold for ourselves (inasmuch as we know we don't have the relational hardware to sustain it) upon all others. My question to myself (and eventually to my friends, pastors, and others) became, "… and is your experience pursuing all of those things so rewarding in your day to day life?" We jump at opportunities to solve problems in other lives because we cannot solve the enigma in our own. Our suffering is real, not just something in our minds.

We feel that in-the-moment rewards should come from the effort of earnestly seeking God, so we continue our urgency. But it's not happening, and we project our resentment. We keep pushing forward, but the still, blobby, cracked picture on the screen isn't moving, and we wonder why God leaves us in this state.

That is why I run from the blazing figure – because I do not trust what I see of him. I know my vision and other senses are compromised, and I fear rejection. What I am left with is the *confusion* of what to do next. The *disorientation* of being turned spiritually upside-down – the God who created us for relationship is the same God I just stepped away from. The *consternation* of knowing my relational hardware is gravely broken and has cost me wonderful experiences with the Lord and his people. The *apprehension* that my present experience is deficient – less-than. The *anxiety* of wondering what it will wrest from my life story in the future. The *hopelessness* of going on with my efforts at relating with God while having broken relate-ability.

And yes, to answer your question, yes – it is twisted, to step away from that figure when in my mind, I know that he is the only one who can provide what I'm looking for. But it is also twisted to earnestly seek after God and yet have an inner experience of darkness – to see God's hand in all the universe and individual lives, but find it difficult to impossible to focus on his movement in real time in my own life. Twisted to have this deep, driven desire to see who God is and relate with him (like he created and designed us for that purpose or something), only to be stymied by that static image where I can't even make out any of the features in the picture.

And yes, resentment is there – I would be dishonest to deny it! Isn't that a natural reaction, though, when something you believe you should have is wrested away from you? So yes, there is some resentment toward a God who is good and well able to reveal himself each time I ask.

The flip side of our brokenness is a sense that God himself is standing opposite to us. Nowhere do I feel this more strongly than when I am trying to pray. I cannot just pray through the wall that stands fast from the weight of who I am and the damage to my ability to relate.

Here's some poetry that strongly resonated with me; look to see if it matches your own experience: "*He has driven me away and made me walk in darkness rather than light. He has made my skin and my flesh grow old and has broken my bones. He has made me dwell in darkness like those long dead. He has walled me in so I cannot escape;*

he has weighted me down with chains. Even when I call out or cry for help, he shuts out my prayer. He has barred my way with blocks of stone; he has made my paths crooked... I have been deprived of peace; I have forgotten what prosperity is. So, I say, 'My splendor is gone and all that I had hoped from the Lord.' I remember my affliction and my wandering, the bitterness and the gall. I well remember them, and my soul is downcast within me."

In all of my journey through the fog, never have I read words that so aptly described what it is like for someone in the fog to try to relate with God. I can hear the question: "Come on, is your situation really that desperate? It's not like you're dying here." But really – when you know, as we do, that all of life depends on God himself sustaining it, and the Bible talks about relating with him and talking with him and hearing from him, is it so hard to imagine that we would speak this way? "Anyone who comes to him must believe that he exists and that he rewards those who earnestly seek him."[15] Ok, I've been earnestly seeking for a long time – where are the rewards in my experience?

If I was looking for these words in scripture, I would have expected to find them in the Psalms. Often, when we experience spiritual malaise, we are instructed to look there for writers of similar experience. Certainly, David did go through troublesome times, and some of that is reflected in his poetry.

But these words are not in the Psalms – they come from Lamentations, chapter 3. It is striking that they would be there – that book is the lament of the prophet who could not turn aside the people of Judah from their sins, and so they were dragged away into exile. And if you read the first two chapters of Lamentations, you might see the echoes of a very fog-like experience – eerie silence where there was once joy, far-off cries for help. Wandering through a now-deserted wasteland, yearning so desperately for a fuller experience of the presence of God – something the author had experienced but was now ripped away.

The people of God were now in exile – and of course their daily subjective experience matched that. Where they had known how to worship God in their land and had a legacy from generations before to pass down to those that followed, they now would have confusion about what to do next. They were in a strange land with strange people speaking strange words – they were disoriented. They had the consternation of knowing that their personal and corporate sins had separated them from God and caused the anger that drove them into exile. The apprehension of realizing their present experience didn't include the voice of God as it had in the past. The anxiety of what they would suffer in their new situation. The hopelessness of returning to their own land and prior experience in their lifetime.

Does that sound familiar? The reasons for our journey in the fog are widely varied, and they may well have nothing to do with our own sins. It can come from habitual sin, and it can come from our upbringing. It can come from things that happen to us or from trauma committed against us. But make no mistake: those of us in the fog are walking through an experience of exile.

Tom Petty said you don't have to live like a refugee,[16] but that is exactly our Christian experience. On paper we know we are all the things in Christ, but day by day our neurons give us very mixed signals. Spiritually speaking, we are far, far separated from the full experience of God's presence that is available even in this life.

We live in a strange land on many fronts – in the world, we see nothing that will fill our inner God-shaped hole. In the church, we feel alienated by quick solutions to our problems (if our experience is heard at all) and the following of a god who can't seem to handle the long-term process of complex human experience. In our families, we can experience rejection of parts of who we are, because family members will be uncomfortable with the idea that they contributed to our experience in some way.

We have searched scripture and sought those who seem to know God, and we have no really good idea of what to do next. And while the long-term process of God's healing may yet bring some of that experience to us, what we have right now is a sense of hopelessness that things will change.

When we are brave enough to voice these ideas aloud, this is the point where people will get tied up in knots. They're reluctant but willing to allow for our lack of obvious joy and some of our descriptions of life in the fog, but here is where they'll draw the line. They turn into Job's friends and start pushing back hard against what we're saying: "It really is starting to sound like you're blaming God for all of this. Are you blaming God? Because you shouldn't – he made you and died for you! He doesn't deserve your anger."

Now, while I struggle daily to relate with God even to the somewhat broken level that I can relate with my fellow human beings, I strongly believe that God is big enough and good enough to handle all that I throw at him. I'm not spending all of this effort to relate with some paper God who is easily torn and shredded by the complexity of my experience. I think it is admirable that our friends are so concerned about God's reputation – but he's a big God, and he can take care of his own reputation.

He has the entire universe declaring his glory, and all I'm asking is for someone to listen to what our experience of following him is like.

8. Attachment

As I continue to wander, I draw toward the light once again. The Blazing Figure has remained for another encounter. I shy away another time, and again and again I cycle through his presence and back into the fog. He takes each of my answers in stride.

My attempts at bandages have brought on infections – he shows me that these makeshift coverings were actually sharp razors. I begin to contemplate my madness – I had been using these all along to help myself. Now, not only am I beaten and bloodied by others, in my insanity I have ripped open my own soul.

There is a peculiar phenomenon in this world: every day, children all over the globe are united with new families. Sometimes, the family of their birth simply can't care for them as they deserve. For others, they were neglected or outright abused by their caretakers and removed by the authorities. Either way, these precious children are entrusted to families who have love to give and resources to provide.

When a family has extra, or at least feels like they can move enough things around to make do, and decides to shelter, feed, clothe, love, and raise another child, this is a wonderful work of the Spirit. And every child who gets this new, dedicated family to themselves is eternally grateful and weeps tears of joy, right? Actually, no... The peculiar phenomenon for the child is that, even though a whole bunch of things are starting to go right for their lives, they are ambivalent, confused, often angry, and will lash out against their new kin.

Children who have experienced adoption – the wonderful inclusion in a new family – have also experienced great loss. They've lost the beginning bonds they had in the womb. In many cases, they've lost the innocence of infancy, in that they've been made to feel frustration and anger over having needs which would not be met. They have the loss of experiencing violence at an age when it completely shapes their comprehension of themselves. And, they have the loss that comes from developing insecure attachments.

Attachment patterns are set in our neural networks and shaped by how we relate with our primary caregivers early in life. They shape how we relate with people throughout life. They are the fundamental building block of the way we experience relationship, and for those of us who are in the fog, they are broken in many ways. We've talked about separation that comes from broken relational hardware – that's a broken attachment style. Some of us have that brokenness just with God. But a lot of us who are in the fog experience this in almost all of our relationships.

Look – we don't need to be adopted children to have insecure attachments, and many of us in the fog have exactly that. We are the Functional Hurting, after all. But let's look at some of the experiences that children will have as they become part of new family units, and then ask ourselves, does that sound like me in my relationships and in the family of God?

They will often be slow to trust their new parents. They will hoard things to give themselves a sense of control, but it will end up hurting them and those around them. They may try to manipulate the new parent to get what they want. Some may try and try and try to please the new parents, but when they don't feel loved, will get frustrated and start to shut down. They can be frantic, not knowing how to deal with all the emotions. After all, being loved and accepted is not the same as feeling loved and accepted.

Does any of that remind you of your fog? Especially when it comes to relating with God – but also with other believers in the church –

we can see some or all of those things. For better or for worse, we often conflate our concept of who God is, with our fathers. Even if we had a good dad, though, we can struggle mightily with relating to the invisible God.

We hear the words God says (by reading them in a book), but we can be slow to trust them because we've not clearly seen the results. We are confused about the character of our new parent. We get ourselves addicted to things, listening to the sirens that call us into the darkness, and they hurt us and those around us. We set up our godly deeds and devotions on a pedestal, as if it should all make God do something more for us.

And, we've tried and tried and tried to please God, but we're in the fog. If we're honest, we can admit we don't feel loved. Our problems with feeling like we are part of the team carry forward into church experience – it seems like we just don't measure up, we're less-than, we're second-class Christians. We've been frustrated. We've started to shut down. We've been running through the fog recklessly – frantic, not knowing where to go or what to do next. Even when coming face to face with the Blazing Figure, who we recognize is the life-giver and the healer, we backed away from him as well and stumbled back into the darkness.

And there's the thing – we who are in the fog are acting like adopted children. And it fits – the Bible tells us that we who come to Christ to deal with our sins, become adopted sons and daughters of God. I've heard a lot of sermons about that adoption. In school, I was assigned quite a bit of reading about what it means and how that flows through our lives and into eternity. There are a lot of positive aspects to be appreciated.

What can be added to all that teaching is a bit of necessary soul-searching. We're being taught a lot of good, true, objective realities that describe who we are in Jesus. But do we then ask ourselves, do I FEEL all of these things? And are those positive aspects all there is to spiritual adoption?

What I didn't see, and what's really quite important to those of us wandering in the fog, was the negative parts of the experience of coming into a new family. For many of us who follow God, the Holy Spirit does not short-circuit the attachment process just because we're saved. When we got born again and started being living, breathing members of the family of God, what was our attachment to God, our parent?

Reflecting back can be helpful, to see how we related with our earthly parents. I think it's possible to be securely attached to our parents while insecurely attached to God, but I also believe it would be rare the other way around. Never count out the supernatural, but the way we relate to our parents can often carry into what we do with God.

We each have a God-image etched into our neural networks that represents God in our brains. Ideally, the way our idea of God acts and reacts is united with the character of God in scripture. But the ideal is rare in the fog, isn't it? Maybe our God-image has been damaged – that would explain the brokenness of how we relate, and how we end up feeling so separated.

Children who grow up without earthly fathers, or who had strained relationships with their earthly fathers, statistically experience far more problems in life.[17] Is it any wonder, then, that those of us who struggle to relate to our heavenly Father experience some of the same in the spiritual realm? Jesus promised rest to the weary, but we who deal with anxiety in the fog every day are not relating to that rest right now. So, we are more vulnerable to our various problems, such as addictions.

We ought to have strong relationship with our divine parent that can include speaking to him about our deepest struggles and longings. Instead, we feel shame and guilt so strongly every time we pray, that we can even dissociate spiritually and stop feeling all heavenward emotions. Without that bond there, is it any wonder that our worries continue, and that our pain persists?

Increasingly, I see myself interact with God as an adopted child, showing insecure attachment. I look for ways to please God, but mind you, this is not out of a deep-seated trust. Instead, I'm anxiously trying to figure out how to get him to love me. Sound twisted? It is! And it's not internally consistent, because I fundamentally believe there is nothing I can do that will make God love me – that has to be up to him.

But I can get fairly obsessive-compulsive about my attempts at relationship: read your Bible every day, or it won't be a good day. Make sure you pray, or you'll never get what you want. No, don't pray for that, or God will give you something else entirely. Pray the right words, or it won't happen. Read the right Bible verses, or you won't learn what you need to learn today. Worship the right way. Sing the right way. Feel the right way.

It's exhausting. OCD Christianity doesn't work, so I isolate myself – I fear continual rejection, so I cope with that by turning away. In a particular form of madness, it makes sense, doesn't it – preclude the hard rejection by just being absent. But the experience of exile comes as I walk away from the Blazing Figure – it is a syndrome of the soul trapped in the fog.

Faults and regrets are amplified. Things that could cause joy are questioned incessantly until they produce quite the opposite experience. Silence is held, and everything is kept at bay in the mind for a while. But eventually the dam breaks, it floods consciousness, and the sorrow is overwhelming.

The cycle continues: the growing anxiety leads to greater efforts, the work to exhaustion, the fatigue to more anxiety – all running around until there is a moment of rest. Not peace, mind you, just a soul-numbing rest where I just don't feel anymore. The rest passes, the soul catches a breath, and then we move back into the same rhythm.

I've observed foster children with this kind of cycle as attachments grew. Some days would seem fine (the rest), but other periods of time would seem driven by pure chaos. When the child was on the up side, you'd hold your breath, because you knew, just *knew* that they'd be cruising for wild behavior next week. And the bad times did come, and it was enormously difficult to remember that things would ever swing upward again.

The pendulum continues ever on for the soul as well. For one, it's hard to enjoy tentative rest when we're told the Christian life can be so much more than that. But that seems to be all we in the fog get for now, and even then, the moment passes on and our souls descend into chaos, where the way back up remains difficult to see.

Each time I go to church, I experience the heightened state of anxiety and the ensuing draw to dissociate and not feel. Every time, I hear words that condemn – not the particular action sins I deal with, but the very daily experience of my soul. The very concept of being part of a group is foreign to me, though the church is supposed to be a place where we haven't earned our place in the group. I never really had that experience when I was growing up.

At some point, I realized that I had to prove my worth for each community I was in. With the kids in Sunday School, I didn't have the current pop-culture and sports knowledge that made me worth talking to. I had few real friends, and I lacked skills and confidence to make new friends. So, I have this idea of what church should be as a place of refuge from "earning" kinds of communities, but it doesn't match my experience.

Then there are the songs. So, so many songs that bring me down. I look around at all the people singing, and I wonder if it's really working for them. Are the words true to their experience? Are they just comfortable with the rhythmic, weekly sing-along? Or are they more like me, disturbed by the exercise? It's usually at least one song a week that will send me into a tailspin, if I let it.

For example, the song, "At the Cross,"[18] speaks of a burden rolling away and concludes, "and now I am happy all the day." Am I? Is that anywhere close to my experience? No. Instead, I anxiously analyze everything to the n-th degree, so that I can draw something of that light out for myself. Look around the room – do I see a lot of happiness going on?

Another song, "In the Garden,"[19] speaks of the joy shared with God himself in time spent walking together. Again – is that my experience? No. I am in this cycle of, on the one hand, wanting to trust, but on the other hand, not seeming to have the capacity to do so.

The sermon brings it home for the full circle. I am already uncomfortable in the group and disturbed by the words of a song, and now I listen to more words that are supposed to teach me how to follow God better. I still believe there is value in listening to the sermons, and I hope that something clicks. There are some things I hold onto for dear life, because a lot of the cyclical anxiety just doesn't seem to go away.

I used to listen to sermons intently, hoping that I'd get that one insight that would snap everything into focus, freeing me to live the life I was always supposed to. But that just doesn't work when the rest of the weekly church experience grinds against all the God-and-people attachment issues I have, and when each song seems to drop a grain of salt in the wounds once more.

We are indeed the adopted children of God. But we are not yet healed.

PART II

9. Word

> Both he who sanctifies and those who are sanctified are all
> from one father, for which reason he is not ashamed to call
> them brethren, saying, "I will proclaim your name to my
> brethren, and in the midst of the congregation I will sing your
> praise." And again, "I will put my trust in him." And again,
> "Behold, I and the children whom God has given me."
>
> Hebrews 2:11-13

Let's take a moment, shall we, to pick our heads up and look around.
The chapters up to here are heavy, aren't they? At least, they are
heavy to those of us who have long walked in the depths of the
fog. We've been having a conversation, starting with, "Yeah, that
is a thing I feel too," then digging a bit at the swirling clouds that
hang about us. The general anxiety. The sounds and voices we hear
around us – indeed also there in the fog. The pain we carry with
us each day – the things that happen to us, and the ways we lurch
toward the false saviors out there that would drag us away.

We've encountered the powerful figure in flame, dazzling in
brilliance in the blur of the fog. He wants to save us, but we resist.
We struggle to trust him, or we're concerned that our journey in
the fog would be without meaning, or we think we need to fix
ourselves. Or, we resented that being with him was not either-or:
the fog would yet persist around us. Something prompted us to walk
away from the one who was speaking words of grace to us, and we
wandered back out into the cold, misty darkness. But we went in
circles, and kept chancing upon this figure – or was he pursuing us?

We had to camp out for a while on the part where we turn away.
For many of us, all our lives we've heard the words of God from

the Bible. We've read them, we've listened to them, we've heard them sung, we've heard them preached, we've sat through Sunday schools. Some of us have been to Bible school, or Christian college, or the seminary. Even with all of that, we step out from the blazing figure's light.

The turning away is fascinating: we show that we are numb to some of the very words of grace that the blazing figure speaks to us. In a way, we've been desensitized to those messages because we've heard them so often, and the dissonance between those words and our lifetime of experience overwhelms us. We'll say all of those words are true, of course – but we psychologically protect ourselves with the unspoken defense: they just aren't true for us.

So, now that we've walked through the separation, and now that we've prodded at attachments a bit to get a handle on our ongoing brokenness, let's rest for a while. Let's take a breath, and see if we can hear some of these words with new ears. The blazing figure, the very same savior, has been speaking these words for thousands of years to all of God's children.

He has seen to it that his words were written down, passed through the ages, and given to us for such a time as this. In our dismay and discomfort in the fog, we've had deafened ears to this voice, and we've feared we missed it. But when we are finally ready to breath and listen, the very same voice speaks the very same words, and we may let them sink down to our souls.

When water erodes the earth, it cuts a path for itself, then seeks its level. The more water that flows on the worn path, the easier it is for future water to go the same way. Our brains work that way too – we hear or read a set of words, and pathways begin to form. Often, we've been trenching these passages for years, or even decades. So, we can do lots of devotions and hear lots of sermons without really making new neural paths.

In these meditations, we want to begin rewiring our brains by bringing honest reaction to the words. We're not going back to reading what "we're supposed to read" and reacting "how we're supposed to react" – not just letting the words touch the side of us we think is more acceptable. Instead, we want to bring our full selves to bear, and let the truth slowly change us to set us free.

Often, when we at last feel ready to hear some words, when our souls do ache for the voice of the savior, and all the other whispers have subsided for a time, we can feel overwhelmed, can't we? Quieting the mind is so much work (or we simply don't know how) that it seems like that brief peace is something that happens to us, rather than a state of mind we've been able to muster.

So, when it does happen that our circumstances and brain chemistry click into gear and we experience solace, we know it's brief, and we don't know when it's coming again. We panic a little bit because we want to hear the words of God, but we just don't know where to start. Ironic, isn't it, to be so accustomed to an anxious or downward pattern that we can barely tolerate moments of peace? We must begin somewhere, though – so here is as good a place as any.

Peace is so fleeting for some of us. Simply reading the Bible can dredge up a lot of anxiety, and that is supremely frustrating. Especially when we've long been taught that the way to get closer to God is in his Bible – our anxiety is keeping us from God, and it feels like there's nothing we can do about it. We don't get away from that feeling or silence it here – we are trying to allow that side of us a voice, while also allowing the Savior to speak. We should not expect epiphany – just experience the message and anything it brings forth in our souls.

Hear the words: "He is not ashamed to call them brethren." Who are we talking about? Well, Jesus, of course, the very same being of light who we've gone in circles with and are just beginning to open our ears a little to hear his voice. But who are the "brethren" that he's not ashamed of?

When we think of Jesus being ashamed of people, our minds can tend outward. We consider the fallen televangelists. There are the pastors who have left their families or abused members of the church. And there are the general hypocrites, who praise God on Sunday but live like hell the rest of the time. We think Jesus should be ashamed of Christians who think they know it all, of Christians who exclude or include the wrong people, of Christians who try too hard to be seen as pious, of Christians who stump for the wrong politician, of Christians who text while driving, and of Christians who use the wrong words when they stub their toes.

The longer we consider it, though, our thoughts inevitably stray back to ourselves. We are the Functional Hurting, after all, and introspection comes naturally to many of us. Is Jesus ashamed of me? Truthfully, it often feels like he should be. I have slogged through this foggy experience for a long time – still waiting for a breakthrough here. And I'm quite certain that I've not always had patience for others walking a similar path.

I can point to a myriad of reasons why I shouldn't be on God's team. Any points I'd raise in my defense just ring hollow. Remember our reaction when we found the blazing figure in the fog – we didn't just think he should be ashamed of us: we acted out that he really was ashamed, and we walked away back into that foggy soup. But that's not what he says, is it?

There are some bands that I don't allow myself to listen to anymore. Don't get me wrong – I'm not going to start shilling for the latest and greatest Christian rock band out there, or begin selling some message about having to only listen to music of faith. A lot of great music gets left behind by those who follow that tack. No, I'm talking about specific music, with words that are just a little, shall we say, too real – words that touch at some of my innermost defenses. One of those songs is by Linkin Park, and it's called "Somewhere I Belong."[20]

It's all in the title, isn't it? The words describe an existential crisis, not unlike the one we've been discussing all along. And they touch on something foundational to human experience: the desire to be someone among somebodies, to be part of the group, to matter. It's "something I wanted all along" – and something that has to be sought out, to be found. And those words reach to the core of my being, to a wound that seems to be older and more raw than most of the others. Listening to that song just once can disturb my soul for days, and it raises the question to the front: do I belong?

Being part of a group is hard. When I was very young, I had a hard time identifying with others. I had few good friends and the general sense that I just didn't quite fit in with all the rest. That was an easy enough experience to validate: I didn't know the music, or the movies, or the video games. I didn't know who the sports stars were. And so, I found myself at the margins, looking for ways in.

Please understand, I'm not talking about cliques here, or bullies either – just generally being part of a class, or a group of people my own age. I don't blame those other kids – they were trying to validate their own experiences, and they gravitated toward others like them, who knew what they knew.

Getting into a group, I found, required that I have some skill of value, or some knowledge. I had to prove worthy of being included, and if I didn't maintain that worthiness, I'd be on the outs again. It's easy enough to try this in church by knowing all the answers in Sunday school, or having a calling from God toward some future work. But that doesn't impress the other kids, just the teachers.

I played the trumpet for years and got pretty good at it, so I was in a youth orchestra. I didn't socially fit in there either, but I could be there because I had a skill. When friendships in childhood are a rare commodity, we learn to act out of fear of losing them. Or, in some ways, we give up.

At some point in your life, you start to notice that you're not getting invited to friends' houses – you're doing all the inviting. You notice that in the college dorm, you're visiting but not being visited. You notice that you're asked to help with a lot of things, but not being helped when you ask. You notice that when you walk into a room full of people, everyone is already in the middle of a conversation and you're the one who's not. You're quite certain that you don't merit breaking into any of those, but no one is inviting you into their circle, either.

Even long-standing friendships can be difficult to maintain. I question my motives when I connect with my friends – do I want something out of the conversation, even if it's just the feeling that someone wants me around for a moment? Feeling wanted and desired should be normal. I shouldn't have to question that need.

But I do question it, because I learned through experience that I, by myself, am not worthy of someone's time. By myself, I'm not the glue that holds a group of friends together. In order to belong, I have to bring something else of value to the table. My ability to feel and function as part of a group has been compromised.

So why, other than for being Mr. Perfect Pants, does Jesus say he is not ashamed of his sisters, his brothers, and all who God has given him? What are his words, that I desperately need to touch my soul and begin to forge new neural pathways? Consider Jesus not on the cross, not in blazing glory, but as the man who is God.

He's not playing these games of excluding the "less-than" Christians so he'll have a better team. He's not impressed by our skills, or by our knowledge. He's operating on a different plane of existence – his father's. He's not like the kids we couldn't connect with in our youth, reaching out for validation and seeking common experiences. He's only concerned with one thing: who is your father? If God is your father, you're being sanctified. And that's the reason he is not ashamed: we're family.

That concept, quite frankly, blows my mind. The very idea that to be in league with Jesus, I can just relax – I'm already there, no special sauce to add. It runs counter to all I have experienced in this life. Look, we've already talked about being uncomfortable in church, among God's people, where I often feel like they, too, ought to be ashamed of me.

But here's Jesus, saying, "in the midst of the congregation I will sing your praise!" He's not fazed by any individual Christian around him. He doesn't stop doing his thing when he sees you there. When he finds himself next to you, he does not hide from God, or feel the need to leave the room, or begin to act condescendingly.

Child of God, no matter what your story is, no matter what your struggles are, no matter what pain you feel like Jesus shouldn't have to bother with, no matter what has dampened your voice, no matter how bad you smell, no matter why you've been stuck in the fog day after day – he is proud to stand next to you when he is praising God his father.

It's easy, though, to picture ourselves as an afterthought there. Jesus is proud to stand and praise God as part of the group, but it's easy to think he would be just as happy without me there. It's a twisted reaction – again, the turning away, the "you don't need me, so I don't need to be here." That's our childhood talking again, our lifelong experience built upon it, and the voices that would have us fade and become invisible.

That's not what Jesus says. He says, "I will proclaim Your name to my brethren." He doesn't just face God, proud that he has some motley collection of Christians around him. He also turns to address us, to see our faces, to look us in the eye. He will speak with us. Not only that, he identifies with each one of us in front of the rest of creation: "Behold, I and the children whom God has given me."

We've learned throughout our lives, either by explicit church teaching or by logical extension, that we ought not find worth in ourselves. And that's true, to the extent that we can't save ourselves and that we can't live well outside of the way God made things to be. But if Jesus is bold enough to speak these words to us, we can be bold to repeat them to ourselves.

Some will protest that these concepts make the gospel about us and take away from it being all about Christ. Well, it is indeed all about Jesus, but it's not *not* about us either, is it? It's certainly not the first time the words of Jesus will make the pious uncomfortable.

So next time you read the Bible, give yourself permission to say, "Jesus is proud to give me these words." Next time you are in church, you can look around and say to yourself, "Jesus is proud to stand with each one of us to praise God." Next time you feel like being invisible, you can remind yourself, "Jesus doesn't shy away from me, and he enjoys seeing me."

Many of us have been hurt in the church, by those whose actions will never be validated by their own pain. Many of us have made bad choices, some with knowledge of the consequences and some without. We have faults, we have wounds, we have sins, and we may walk in and out of the fog many days of our lives. We'll struggle onward to find any place on this earth where we feel that we belong, that we matter.

Our voices may still come out as a harsh whisper. But we will have these words that will begin to cancel out our shame.

You are my hiding place and my shield;
I wait for Your word.

Depart from me, evildoers,
That I may observe the commandments of my God.

Sustain me according to Your word, that I may live;
And do not let me be ashamed of my hope.

Psalm 119:114-116

10. Hope

This I recall to my mind,
  Therefore I have hope.

The Lord's lovingkindnesses indeed never cease,
  For His compassions never fail.

They are new every morning.

Words of hope are wonderful to remember, and the scriptures are full of them. Through both Old and New Testament, the God of all creation reveals himself as the God of hope. With hope, we look ahead to eternity: past a long, full life to being present with the Lord. With hope, we also set our sights on lesser goals: we hope for a good family, a profitable job, or a nice vacation.

Whatever we hope for, unless it is pure fantasy (which is quite a different thing), that hope has to have a target – something or someone to hope in, that will bring the hope to life and reality. For those of us in the fog, those targets are hard to see and identify, aren't they? The fog is deep, it is pervasive, and it swirls around each and every part of our lives.

The fog attends church with us. The fog hitches a ride along to our jobs. The fog presses on us in the morning, and keeps us awake at night. Each morning, do you see and feel fresh grace from God above? Or do you see clouds swirling around all the circumstances you dwell in every day?

A lot of us will probably start feeling shame and judgment just reading that. But remember our goal here: to begin retraining how we approach the Word in a way that promotes honest reactions. We are rewiring our brains, slowly but surely.

Feeling judgment in this way is the soul's way of trying to divide itself. It's an uncomfortable feeling, so we'll try to cut off the part of ourselves that causes it. Here, though, instead of immediate action, recognize the feeling for what it is: a sign that we've found a place that our souls need to be put back together. Then we can bring all of ourselves to the text and find fresh reactions.

Hope is more difficult for some of us, depending on the hoped-for object and our history with it. For instance, when putting up an item for sale, some people can expect a buyer will come calling soon. It seems like it comes naturally to them, like they have the golden touch. I learned otherwise, for myself – I haven't had many positive experiences there... Eventually, I learned to just not get my hopes up.

Some people can hope for a successful job in their chosen field, hunt around for a while, and find exactly what they were looking for. Others, not so much. I spent time in the seminary and got to know a lot of students. Some of them were able to find jobs as pastors, even of large churches. Others, and this is hard to watch, saw their hopes of being a pastor come to nothing. They had spent their time and their money training for a job that they couldn't find.

As one of the Functional Hurting, I may struggle to drum up much in the way of hope that the hurting will go away. After all, I've walked in the fog for a long time, so I have taught myself not to hope it will go away any time soon. And that's the thing with hope in the fog: we've taught ourselves not to.

We've had enough days of being down, or anxious, or feeling trapped, or generally not feeling in touch with reality. We aren't getting our hopes up anymore. It's a conditioned response, and one that's now deeply set in our neural networks. In the Christian life, though, we've been taught that hope is a measuring stick for our faith – that if I would just believe the right things, hope should flow from the well of my soul.

Obviously, that hasn't been happening, so the fog comes out as that persistent, nagging notion that I am less-than – that I am a second-class Christian. The good, faithful Christians are over there, where they should be, having their faith-fueled hope and experiencing fresh grace and mercy from God every morning. I am less, and I should not distract them from their life and mission.

That becomes the job I consign to myself in the church: don't trip up the good ones! I must not bring them down with my hopelessness! I must not discourage them! If that means I keep my questions to myself, so be it. If that means I suffer in silence when everyone else in the church is sharing wonderful testimonies, so be it. Sure, God made and meant promises to his people, of abundant life and the like, but clearly the benefits are just not for me in this life.

But in doing that, we've done two things that will end up haunting us. For one, we're isolating ourselves, even if we're still attending church. Few realities are more disheartening than feeling alone when lots of people are around. Because we're staying out of the way of the good ones, we're limiting our interaction with them. And, if God is truly in them and working through them, we're cutting ourselves off from opportunities for healing grace. Second, we end up simply reinforcing the neural networks we've developed, that are telling us we're less-than.

A while ago we talked about exile: God's people, who were not in any way, shape, or form following him, were conquered by an ungodly nation and dragged off into a foreign land. They'd had all the benefits of God's promises, but they sinned so frequently and willfully that they messed that up. No more did they have the temple for worship. No more did they have their safe cities. No more did they have the land familiar to them. In its place, they found themselves in a situation where they existed at the whim of strange people, with weird customs and everyday practices, in a place most of them had never seen before.

But it wasn't just the ones who sinned, either, that ended up in that foreign land of exile. They had children born to them in that time. Those kids weren't trapped in exile through any fault of their own – they were just unlucky enough to be born that way. That was the entirety of their experience, throughout childhood. For them, they hadn't seen the promised land. They hadn't experienced worship in the temple.

But they were not so far removed – they learned what they were missing from all the stories they were told. So, we see both in this strange land: the people who messed up and got dragged there, and the ones who without so much fault just happened to wake up there. Both had the promises of God to their people, and both experienced deprivation.

Picture it this way: you've had to travel to an area that's unfamiliar, and you need to find a particular house without an address or GPS. You'd feel pretty disoriented. Roads don't always go where you think they should, and if there's no GPS giving you step-by-step directions, you get lost. Dusk is falling, and you know that at night, it will be harder to see. The fog descends and swirls around. You would get out to ask for help, but you've done that a few times and no one would talk to you.

You finally find someone that seems to want to help, so you ask a couple of questions. He looks at you quizzically, shrugs his shoulders, and then speaks some words in a gibberish you don't understand. You are a stranger in a strange land, and you don't know how to get where you need to go. And you know that God promised you something about a land way over there, where people speak the language you understand – but it's so far away.

Doesn't that sound exactly like how we are living the life of following Jesus? We've been taught that the Bible gives us answers for life's questions, but we seem to just get more questions. We've been taught that we should find friends, peace, and rest in the church, but we feel like a fish out of water.

We know our questions are unanswered or unwelcome – and that what we feel about our walk with God separates us from many within those walls. We've been taught that we are aliens and strangers in this world, since our home is in the world to come – and that truth we feel fully in tune with! So, we feel trapped between two worlds – we find ways to function in both without really belonging in either one.

The experience of exile – that's what we are living, and that's where we're stuck. So was the one who wrote those words above – Jeremiah, the prophet. Now, that was a man who God told to say some unpopular things, and people didn't listen. So those people got dragged into that foreign, strange land. The prophet didn't, in fact, get hauled off with them – their captors allowed him to stay behind.[21]

At first glance, that seems like it wouldn't be so bad, since he got to be in the place he knew. But almost everyone was gone, so he was left walking around towns and cities that were almost silent, like those movies that portray the "last man on Earth." Even though he was in a familiar land, he didn't have the familiar experience of the land, so he had that experience of exile too.

Jeremiah's words throughout the book of Lamentations are valuable for us, the Functional Hurting. They give us a vocabulary that doesn't come naturally. They give voice to a part of us that has been silenced for too long. Reading through that book with dry eyes is almost impossible for me. Something always resonates with an inner wound or pain. He even talks about his prayers getting shut out – the man who had such close communion with God before, no longer had the same kind of access. How often have you felt like your prayers were bouncing off the ceiling?

We get stuck – we who are in the fog and having this experience of exile – because we continue to bear the effects of an ongoing trauma. For the people of God living in Babylon, they knew (once they got through a stage of denial) that the exile would not be over quickly. They had to settle in to the idea that each morning, they would wake up in an unfamiliar, disorienting place. Jeremiah had the land, but not the people: every day, he'd open his eyes to a postapocalyptic land, eerily quiet.

For both, in order to survive, part of their psyches would want to settle in and get used to it. Another, very loud part of their minds didn't want anything of the sort – to assimilate would mean to give up everything that made them a distinctive people who had God's promises. We see in the Bible that some fell on either side of that psychological divide. The daily blows of reality and that inner splitting combined to inflict a trauma that went on for most or all of their lives.

So, what about us? Well, part of us is indeed used to (or getting accustomed to) the fog, this strange land that we're wandering around. And the other side of us, which is loud in our minds but not often voiced, is shouting that we ought not be here at all – that God intended something better for us than this disorienting, disillusioning existence. But we have to function where we are, don't we? And where we reside existentially is that very place of cloud and shadow.

To make it through the days, to tone down the lows, we also tone down the highs. In the interest of survival, we endure the ongoing trauma by making ourselves as numb as possible. Our unspoken experience causes us to hide – unspoken because we don't want people to know we're in the fog. They must not know, because we find that threatening. We have enough trouble taking care of ourselves, without having to fend off even those who would mean well but don't understand our experience.

Or, we're stuck on the other side of that psychological divide. What's here is something that's driven by the same ongoing trauma, but takes a different tack on coping. Instead of self-numbing, this is the part of the psyche that shouts the content of the hope – all the things that ought to be true now, or will be true someday. Where we are is not where we are supposed to be, so we should get on with living where we're supposed to be already.

To function there, we have to be more suggestible, and we more easily reinterpret our experiences to fit the framework we think they're supposed to. For instance, the hope is that I will have a fulfilling church experience, since the promise is that (eventually) we will be united and operating in harmony. That reality is yet to come in whole, but being stuck in an experience of exile, and being stuck on that side of the psyche, I would act in ways that attempt to reflect that reality before it comes to fruition.

There are lots of ways that comes out: I may deal harshly with those I deem troublemakers. I may seek to correct every wrong I see so that ultimate reality comes faster. I may round up every willing soul for "kingdom work." Or, perhaps I treat others as I treat myself – focusing so hard on making the hope real that I silence their wounds and pain.

This is the road of exhaustion. In my experience and from those I've been able to observe, you can do this for a few years, but it will come crashing down. Living in the fog takes a lot of energy just to achieve or maintain some type of equilibrium, so we don't have the reserves necessary to go about changing the world. Many leaders dwell here, driven by a sense of insufficiency and the desire to make whole all that surrounds them.

For the long haul, we fog-dwellers have trained ourselves not to hope. We do know how to look forward, for certain. But we've seen what it takes to survive in this world of ours – whether it's the consequences of our past decisions, horrible acts done to us, something awry in our brain chemistry, or gut microbes just throwing things off. We have seen months and years come and go, and we have begun to understand that this experience of exile doesn't just go away.

We may have times of respite, but overall, we see the patterns and know that we're not just going to snap our fingers and will it all away. So, our experience pressures us to act through the motions, to keep quiet, and to assume that life will continue in a certain direction. Nightly we discipline ourselves not to hope too highly for the morning, because the same relational baggage we have today will be there tomorrow.

Do we hope at all? Of course, we do – we just put the object of that hope quite a bit further out in the future. All of God's promises that we aren't actively experiencing – those have to be for some time, some place, some next-level reality that isn't here. It's easy enough to look around and see Christians who by all accounts are getting some of the benefits of those promises here and now. But for us, by and large, it's just not there. So, we can either feel that pain of loss, or find ways to numb ourselves to it.

Have you ever had a painful sickness, and wished you could just sleep until you got better? Or maybe you've binge-watched a show (or eight) feeling like when you were done, maybe the world around you would have finally moved on and figured something out.

That's the reason we go for the false saviors. That's why we fall into addictions and get hooked on the drugs, the alcohol, the pornography, the eating disorders, the self-harm, name it. Someday the promise gets fulfilled, and we want to be there then – but we'd rather not experience the fog for as long as it takes to get there, thank you very much. But that's just that one side of our psyche, the one we've allowed ourselves to be aware of most frequently.

There are few things we need more, though, than for once to have the voice of that other side heard, along with the weeping that goes with it. In the name of survival, remember, we fell on one side of the divide – the one that allowed us to function longer-term. The other side we may have tried for a while, and by itself the experience was tiring. But that other side is still there – it gets mad because we silence it. It gets sad because we refuse to listen to it. And once in a while, it gets really mean and causes us a special angst and consternation, because it will not be ignored.

We don't have trouble with hope because we're anti-hope. No, not at all. Rather, hope resides in the part of our subconscious which realizes that where we are is messed up, we're not where we should be, and we'll certainly (eventually) end up somewhere else. And that voice is being choked back by unexpressed, repressed sadness built up by a lifetime of survival. The answer is not to continue to favor one side or strategy of the psyche over the other, but to start learning how to put them together.

Be aware, though, when we finally pull the cork that's holding all of that sadness back, a massive wave of pent-up sorrow gets unleashed, and that can be pretty scary. Having a good therapist close by can be of immense help to put some structure around that wave – or at least someone who is acquainted with the ways the fog can tear at wounds and leave scars in our minds and souls.

When you hear the words, "His mercies are new every morning," or, "I look forward to close, daily companionship with Jesus," do you feel somewhat accomplished yet tired? Do you feel nothing? Or do you weep? For those of us in the fog, that's a fairly accurate barometer of where we are – we can have an idea, at least, of whether we're falling on one side of the divide, the other, or if we've begun to bind the two together. We who are in the fog don't get a map of the way out, but we can find ways to get unstuck and move forward.

If we're actively numbing ourselves through some kind of addiction, we're not actively hoping. Instead, we're silencing that hope until it finally comes to fruition. We want to enjoy the result without experiencing the looking forward.

Passively training ourselves not to hope is our method of survival

– being stuck in a mind-loop where only our current existence is allowed into the picture. We can act like that's all life will ever be. Those here can be the addicts who are whiling away the days and years.

Or, counter-intuitively, these are the more functional of the Functional Hurting – those of us going through life responsibly, and even taking pride in how much we have accomplished, given the existential crisis that dogs us in so great a portion of our lives. We're letting life happen to us passively, or we've made survival our business – either way, we silence hope as a threat, for by showing us another reality, it would disturb the careful balance we've built for ourselves.

Perhaps you're on the other side – doing everything in your power to will that hope into reality. If so, how is that working out for you, in your church, in your marriage, in your parenting, in your friendships? For those stuck in the rat race of maintaining an over-realized hope, please slow down! I know you think you can't let go, that you shouldn't, that you mustn't. If you do, you know that like a spinning top that slows down, you'll fall over.

All of that effort, all of the getting up the gumption, and all of the pressing others around you to perform – it will all seem for naught. And what are you left with but the disillusionment of not knowing where to go next? You must slow down. Our true hope is that we have a savior who will bring the promises to pass, and you are silencing that hope by trying to do it yourself and set the timing yourself, making yourself your own savior and one for those who you are able to wrangle into behaving.

And then there is the weeping. The more I walk through the fog, the more I weep. I gain awareness of my loss, the experiences and relationships I fail to have because I never had the opportunity or do not have the relational hardware. I see the depth of distinction between the already and the not yet. So yes, I weep.

Someone, somewhere gave us the impression that hope should make us happy. On the contrary, hope gives us harmony. Hope takes us away from being stuck in some point in space, and puts us on a line – I was somewhere, now I am here, and in hope I can look ahead to where I am going. As we allow hope to speak, we will see more clearly how the fog blinded us, how we have been stuck, and also how we will continue to experience some aspects of the fog.

So, we weep, but this is a much healthier place to be: we know the past and how it has led us here, and yet the future is still out there for us. We can function in the day-to-day living of life while allowing ourselves to contemplate the coming fulfillment of the promises. We can share our awareness of the imperfect while staying grounded in the knowledge of our limitations.

Keep in mind what hope we signed up for when we started following Jesus: some fulfillment in this life, but most in the next. As some are healed of medical maladies in this life, but all in the next, we can hold onto the same words of life abundant, but shift the time. We can't just check out of this life, not be faithful, and also expect to get the full benefit of the blessing in the next life. So, for those of us in the fog, our hope remains grounded in our daily life – not in fulfillment, but in preparation.

Life goes on and our loss continues at present, but hope remains: Jesus has a place he is preparing, and God's mercies are new every morning.

Why are you in despair, O my soul?
And why have you become disturbed within me?

Hope in God, for I shall again praise Him
For the help of His presence.

Psalm 42:5

11. Garden

> *For we do not have a high priest who cannot sympathize with our weaknesses, but One who has been tempted in all things as we are, yet without sin.*
>
> *Hebrews 4:15*

Temptation. We deal with it almost all our lives, don't we? We start knowing it when we're small children, as the impulse to do the wrong thing. The voice that tells us it would be better for us to lie instead of telling the truth. The inkling in our minds that we ought to take that cookie when Mommy said not to. The force of rage within us that drives us to use our fists instead of our words.

Then we grow in age and nuance, and we discover temptation can be more subtle: do we use kind or unkind words? Do we help or hinder? Do we do the good we know we should do?

We grow into adulthood, and we figure out that temptation runs far deeper still: are our thoughts and actions honoring our relationships with God and others, or are we just looking out for number one? We begin to sort out what wisdom for life looks like.

For the Functional Hurting in the fog, these are the sorts of questions where the picture gets murky, the room starts spinning, and we lose track of where we are. The kinds of neural pathways we've developed are not leading to an integrated or helpful experience of life and spirituality. We need to approach the subject of temptation in a way that, over time, can start wearing in new paths.

Dissecting motivation can be tricky, when our experience of

boundaries is an unsettled one: of the motivations I see, which one is mine? And which is the one I was told to have? The reality is that we live both proactively and reactively. We have a proactive, practiced regimen of defense mechanisms that help us to function in everyday life, but we have a lot of thoughts and actions that are more raw: reactions to all that we see around us.

We have to have that purposeful routine, because without it, our lives in the fog tend toward chaos. It is possible (ideally) for us to take our reactions, observe them, and deal with them in a resourceful manner. Most often, though, we aren't able to do that right away. In the moment, these reactions define our reality, such that our vision, hearing, and other senses are captivated by them. A hurtful word, a trigger of a past memory, a threat of losing something of value – all of these (and more) can lead to reactions outside of our practiced routine.

Some of us were taught that reaction is bad – or even shameful. We continually got the message that we should not get angry when we were treated in certain ways, or that we should not be sad about events that unfolded. Emotions are tools, we heard, and we have to learn to control them.

And while unchecked emotions can certainly be problematic, we ended up feeling the need to stop every reaction in its tracks, interrogate it soundly, and then either stifle it or allow it in a more tempered intensity. If you were told how to feel as well as how to think and act, you were not just instructed in proactive methods to function in this world. Instead, you were also taught that relationship is too fragile for genuine reaction.

Isn't it both interesting and tragic that words spoken just once can define our stories for years? The human soul can be fragile, it can be wounded, and it can be fractured. At each one of those breaks, there is an inner, existential pain that no drug can touch, and anything pressing on those wounds and raw spots will get us to react. When we react, things can get ugly, very quickly. Many times, the cycle continues and multiplies: we react to our own wounds being painful, and wounded souls continue to wound each other.

Drawing lines in the fog can feel futile. Is the impulse to react a temptation? Are the reactions themselves sin? I see no reason to thrust an equals sign between those, but the longer we walk in the fog, the more we need to realize that almost all dichotomies are false as well. The pain itself is not temptation, but temptation is likely present in the moment. The reaction may not be all sinful, but that doesn't mean that there are no sinful elements around it.

The reason those lines matter, though, is that we like to keep score. We like to think that we can measure, from hour to hour and day to day, whether we're better or worse than we were before. Or, we like to think we can ascertain whether we're a better person than Joe at work or Amelia at church. Is my experience of the Christian walk better or worse than theirs?

In other words, we're approaching relationship with God and others as a zero-sum game where single units of sin and temptation matter in the grand totals. Often, we do this because we were taught that herein lies discipleship and godliness, in measurement and improvement. Many churches have their people live this way, and they encourage it by teaching that salvation itself is tied up with that ongoing performance.

Perhaps they teach that you can't be saved unless you start cleaning up your act at the same time. Other churches will teach that you never were saved to begin with, unless you are continually improving in your spiritual and relational walk with God and others. Or, they may teach that salvation may be lost by those who are careless. In any case, such churches often do not develop distinctions between wound and sin.

Those messages of quantification can resonate with us, for a while. We walk in a realm where few things are clear, where disorientation reigns: of course, we'll grab onto something that seems measurable and attainable to give our lives some sense of meaning, hope, and significance. We find a way of life that is satisfying, simple, and gives labels to inner experiences that before had just brought us chaos.

But as we distract ourselves from the fog with a system and try to bring order to a realm of chaos, the cracks start to show. We were given a way to deal with temptation, and we had to pretend that it was a way to deal with pain as well. We were trained to work on our sins as much as possible, and then also told to deal with our baser reactions the same way.

For simplicity's sake, we looked at our lives like we'd been blind in one eye – no depth perception. We had a single facade to evaluate, sin or no sin, and the depth of soul experience behind it could be ignored. But our subconscious does not allow that – it fights back to be noticed. That depth of experience, history, and woundedness wants to be heard. The result: we feel guilty for our reactions to pain, whether sinful or not.

We feel shameful for having this pain to begin with. Often, as we look back, we feel that if we had just been stronger sooner, we wouldn't have had these wounds. Looking forward, we feel fearful that we will never be able to resolve some of these "sins" and move on with discipleship.

If your right hand causes you to sin, cut if off.[22] If your pain causes you to "sin," it gets cut off (or ignored) too. Does the pain disappear, or does it just keep pressing on the system until it comes screaming out once again? We are not skilled surgeons, we in the fog, and we are liable to sequester pieces of our souls that God would have us retain.

The simple system works for a while, though, as long as we don't question every motive, every thought, every action. For those of us who are more insight-oriented or introspective, the whole idea burns down quickly, because trying to keep score soon shows us the futility of doing so. Every aspect of our lives can be questioned *ad nauseam.* If we are unwilling to give ourselves the benefit of the doubt, none of it will stand up to scrutiny.

Confusion led us to take up that version of discipleship at the start. This fresh letdown dumps us now into a deeper distress than before. But as the smoke clears, we see the more familiar confusion and disorientation of the fog: our wounds were never healed or even dressed, our pain never assuaged. We were simply on one of the fog's long, circular side paths.

Lest we despair at taking the long way around (again), we do have more data and (hopefully) wisdom for navigating the misty realm. Systems that address only sin, or only wounds, and reduce all experience to labels in those categories will not resolve things for us. For certain, we may learn valuable lessons on those side journeys, and we may meet lifelong friends. But in the end, the system did not match the depth of reality, and we have to move on.

Remember the reason we went down that path: it resonated with us by giving us a temporary distraction from the pain. We in the fog have a lot of deep, inner pain. We guard our wounds both consciously and subconsciously (that is, with proactive and reactive methods), because we do not want our pain to be part of our present reality. We don't want to feel that existential pain, because it tears into the nerves of our souls.

We take on simple systems because they promise to divert us in our darkest times in the fog, when the entirety of our painful existence bears down upon us. In those hours, we remember the pain of the past, we observe the chaos and pain around us in the present, and we peer with dark, obscured vision down the tunnel of the future to see what pain we can project there as well. What possible human response is there but despair to a lifetime of inner pain? The contemplation of it is overwhelming.

On occasion, I have witnessed partial solar eclipses. When we think of an eclipse of the sun, usually, we're picturing the total blocking of the light. We've seen the images, where the moon is completely in front of the sun and appears as a black circle surrounded by a brilliant corona. But if we move some miles away from where the moon would be exactly in front of the sun, it only takes out part of the light. Then, we're seeing a partial eclipse.

It's a weird light, that seems at the same time to be too bright and too dim, making it hard to focus. Though shining in a clear sky, the sun feels unsettling and wrong. We walk through the fog for so long and are oppressed by it for so long, and then we have those times when those inner clouds finally break. A strange light, like that of the partial eclipse, shines through without depth in an ominous manner.

In that light, we see all of our pain and suffering at once: all of our sour memories, bad experiences, and wounds. They seem very present in that moment – not memories of the past, like they should be, but present experience all over again, where we do and experience the same things again. When all of that experience congeals together, we can't handle that, and inwardly we start retching.

We stay there in the strange light without fleeing, though, because we've seen enough stories of climax and catharsis that we think that sort of path is our only hope of relief. We think that if all our pain gets compounded together, comes to a head, and if we deal with it in a single moment, we'll suddenly "get it" and experience a rushing sense of cool, hopeful, refreshing peace – or at least relief.

In those moments that we try, we're often searching for that one simple truth or lesson to be learned that would make all the pain make more sense. We want that breakthrough moment of coming out of the grey, wispy clouds into the warm, bright, uneclipsed sun. If I just hang on in this moment a little longer, we think, I'll finally achieve that spiritual quantum leap.

Many Christian writers over the years and centuries have written of moments like these, particularly with respect to prayer. If you want the blessing, they say, you must persevere through that inner battle, wrestle with God as Jacob did, and see it through to the end. For those in the fog who are hyper-aware of what is wrong with us, though, that leaves us in a dark place with a puzzle that cannot be solved. That is, did I fail to achieve the breakthrough due to lack of faith, lack of persistence, or lack of alignment with God's will?

The journey is not a matter of having enough faith to deal with all of our pain, or having the right prayers, or staying in a dark state of mind long enough. We cannot deal with all our pain at once. It is impossible, for doing that is to experience the entirety of our being at once, which is excruciating and quite probably the essence of hell.

There is a song that many of an older generation will recognize, that I've mentioned before. In that song, "In the Garden,"[23] walking with God is described as spending time with him in a garden. It is a narration of inner joy, of ways that all of the lyricist's senses are harmoniously in relationship with the God of the garden.

The writer hears God's voice toward him concerning his status and reality, and that voice remains audible even when the garden is left behind for a time. It is a song of restoration meant to invoke thoughts of how Adam and Eve walked with God in the garden of Eden prior to falling into sin. And it is meant as an encouragement to accept that restoration in our personal walks with God.

We see in the church, at least in the evangelical variety, a common teaching and the pressure to follow it: the expectation that we will function as if we are in a renewed garden of Eden. Peaceful, harmonious relation with God is to be found there. Do all you can, they say, to get to that state of being, where you have that relational experience with God. If you don't have that, you're missing something.

They'll tell you that everyone in that garden has the same type of salvation experience – they walked the aisles, they raised their hands, they prayed that prayer, and they all experienced a relief in their souls. They've followed the discipleship path, and heard God's voice – if you'll just follow the program, you'll hear it too!

If the garden experience for the writer was indeed what he describes in those lines, I say, good for him. For many of us in the fog, hearing that song is a constant reminder that we are far from that reality. We get trained by the message of the song, by the sermons we've heard, by the Bible studies we've been a part of, and by general conversations: unless we have these more joyous, meaningful spiritual experiences, there is something wrong with us. And if our more natural context is an experience of exile or the notion of hell itself as we get overwhelmed by the pain of raw soul-wounds, that song was written for the wrong garden.

In Eden, God was with his created humanity in harmony. He walked tall with his people, they walked tall with him, and their perception of his glory was clear. Eden is the expectation from what we have been taught, and it is how spirituality was described to us: if we read our Bibles more, if we pray more, if we do more of all the things, if our spirit is in the right place, then we will experience benefits and blessings.

Where we are in this fog, though, discord reigns, clear sight is far from us, and we lie on our faces rather than standing upright. We hesitate to ask questions, because our experience and awareness seem a threat to the status quo. We fear that we are Adam and Eve in the garden *after* the fall: fearful of being discovered for what we are and cast out.

Strife, confusion, disorientation, and anxiety have no meaning in pre-fall Eden. By the time Adam and Eve felt these things, their experience of exile was fast becoming reality. The end of Eden, for those in the fog, is fear, exile, and isolation – the opposite of abundant life.

Let's pull on another thread, from the words in the verse we're meditating on: "We do not have a high priest who cannot sympathize with our weaknesses, but One who has been tempted in all things as we are." These words point us to Jesus, as the new and final high priest over God's people. These words say he can help us because he was tempted as well.

Where was Jesus tempted? Well, we see the titular temptations of Jesus in the wilderness, as Satan directly attempted to make the son of God stray from his path. He never did stray, and it can seem like those temptations are described within an emotional vacuum, and we don't have much to examine there. I hardly think they were not emotionally-charged experiences, but it does not seem to be the point of those texts.

However, Jesus was also tempted in another place. Far from conversing with the devil, as it happens, this time he is talking with God in a garden. We've seen that sort of thing before, with Adam and Eve in Eden, but this time it's different: the garden is not paradise, and Jesus is not walking tall. In this place, Jesus was letting down some of his boundaries.

Here, the existential pain of humanity was entering Jesus' conscious experience as his own pain. As we get overwhelmed when we contemplate the amount of pain and wounds we have experienced, Jesus saw the same as he considered the full weight of not just my pain, but yours and the rest of humanity's also. He also began to realize that his human relationships were about to break down catastrophically, as he would be betrayed and deserted by many closest to him. And he understood that his God-ward relationship would be broken down as well, on the cross itself.

Most often in this garden, Gethsemane, we observe Jesus there during the season of Lent, on Good Friday, in commemoration of the events that led to the cross. When we do, we're usually looking at a single portion of his words: "Not my will, but yours." That choice is the foundation of our salvation – of course we are right to employ careful, singular focus on that point.

We say the rest of the words, and we'll even discuss them a bit. But we seldom sit for any length of time on the experience of Jesus as he interacted with God at that time in his life. Staying on the choice Jesus makes allows us a certain distance from the painful reality of that moment, which can be overwhelming. In doing so, though, we can overlook and underappreciate the perspective of the son of God: his emotional state.

What we see in Jesus in the garden is a pleading with God himself to spare him this excruciating experience: "Take this cup from me!" We see him sweat drops of blood as his focus is drawn to the totality of human experience at once, with all of the sins, wounds, pains, and suffering, which is excruciating and quite probably the essence of hell.

The Functional Hurting in the fog, as aware as we are of pain, are closer to hell in our experience than we are in reality. For Jesus, it became very real: all of that pain of human experience came crashing down upon him on the cross. Where we are unable to realize our inclination to make our own pain climax into peace, He did that all in the time from this garden to the cross, and peace did begin to flood the cosmos.

So, we have the right plot in our minds, that both sin and pain need to be resolved. But often, we have the wrong players on the stage, thinking that we need to be the ones to resolve them. We know that Jesus has taken on our sin. What we see in the garden, though, is that he has also assimilated our pain.

He reacted to that pain by asking God to take the experience away from him, just as we do. He was able to process that reaction and proactively shift the message, but the sameness in his experience allows him to sympathize with our weakness. He knows we are overwhelmed, and he understands the fog we are walking through.

Which garden is your experience? Which are you trying to function in? For those in the fog, Gethsemane is our predominant experience

– not Eden. In our most raw moments, we end up weeping tears, we have strong bouts of anxiety, and we experience the angst of our souls as the sheer weight of our existence bears down upon us. We lose sleep and expend vast amounts of energy to stabilize our experience.

We keep trying to function in Eden, though, because we still really want that to be true for us. We want all our hard work to pay off – the Bible study, the self-examination, the hours in prayer. Why can't we have that experience of God's voice, harmony, peace, and fellowship like those other Christians do? Why do they get to see the light, while our vision is clouded with darkness?

And the what-ifs: what if I only need to persevere a few more days, or a week, to get the breakthrough I've longed for? What if I give up right before the payoff, and miss out? The thought of giving up seems like a threat, like it will upend a system that we perceive to be fragile because it has not rung true for us.

It is psychologically difficult to let go of Eden. Many of us have been taught that paradigm all our lives – that we are either in or out, good enough or not, and that we will miss out if we don't shape up. For some of us, the paradigm has been in force for generations, and that's hard to shake. We hear it from family, from our friends, in our churches – and each is validating the others.

It is okay (really, it is!) for our spiritual siblings to have the experiences they do. And it is fine for them to validate each other as they try, in their own lives, to navigate what it looks like to follow Jesus. If Eden is the complete picture, though, we are left with no one to blame but ourselves for not having the same spiritual experiences as our brothers and sisters – hearing from God, the mountaintop times, and so on. Being focused on the results keeps us from questioning the premise and becoming aware of the unfair expectations being laid on us. The cognitive dissonance will come through, though, as our subconscious calls out against the weight.

Hear this: there is no shame in Gethsemane. If the sinless Jesus went there, certainly we can too. If Jesus pleaded with God to take away painful and excruciating experience, we can too. If Jesus expected (and he did) that God may allow the experience to continue, we can too.

But we know that our experience is tied up with Jesus in the garden and on the cross, which can begin to free us of our impulse to keep score. If we don't need to keep score with our fellow Christians, we don't have to feel like we are missing out on essential experiences. Our experience, while within the same gospel boundary lines, can be entirely different.

Sometimes we can feel like life is a giant, cosmic-scale buildup to a misfire, like it is inevitably a waste of time and space. We feel like we're trying to set up spiritual fireworks – that every prayer, every Bible study, every devotional, every witnessing experience, etc., will add to the powder. Someday, we think, the fuse will be lit, and all of that work will burst forth in beautiful light and shape. Surely, we think, that breakthrough experience will bring glory to God!

Then we feel like the fog is dampening the powder, and we haven't been lit yet. Or that we have been lit, and the dampness made it all fizzle out. But the point of life is not to be spectacular or to be one of the "super-saints" – many of us can't handle the pressure that would come with that anyway. If we trade Eden for Gethsemane, we don't have to worry about any of that. We can simply exist in God's presence.

If we encounter Jesus in Gethsemane, he is with us in temptations. And he is with us in the pain. He understands our experience and sympathizes with our weakness. He's dealing with our sins, and he's working with our reactions. Our conscious existence is affected, and Jesus makes inroads into our subconscious too.

Over time, he may rewire some of the neural networks that hold us in the mist from day to day. We're not walking with him in the garden – we can't even stand up under the weight of our experience. We are on our faces in the grief of our pain and loss, with our experience of exile.

He is right there on the ground with us. He validates our experience and lays the foundation for our hope. Time spent with Jesus there is never wasted.

Since we have confidence to enter the holy place by the blood of Jesus, by a new and living way which He inaugurated for us through the veil, that is, His flesh, and since we have a great priest over the house of God, let us draw near with a sincere heart in full assurance of faith.

Hebrews 10:19-22

12. Truth

> For indeed Jews ask for signs and Greeks search for wisdom;
> but we preach Christ crucified, to Jews a stumbling block and
> to Gentiles foolishness, but to those who are the called, both
> Jews and Greeks, Christ the power of God and the wisdom of
> God. Because the foolishness of God is wiser than men, and the
> weakness of God is stronger than men.
>
> 1 Corinthians 1:22-25

Having grown up in the USA, the land of opportunity and free
speech, I have a favored saying to proffer to those with whom I
disagree: "It's a free country. You have the right to be wrong." It's
pithy, and probably not original to me, but I've been using it for so
long that it seems like my own.

When I say it, I'm running a power play – I am shutting down the
discussion by declaring my conversational companion to be willfully
wrong. Wrong facts I can fix, but wrong will is a bridge too far –
a lost cause not worth pursuing further. It is truly a wonder that
anyone likes me...

Many of us (apparently including me) have a fairly neurotic need to
always be right. We can trace that need to many sources, but we
take great pride in having that firm grasp on how the world works.
Now there is nothing wrong, of course, in having knowledge and in
knowing how to apply it. What we're talking about here is a core
identity rooted in rightness, where the stakes are much higher.

In those rare times that we actually allow ourselves to be proven
wrong, we get disillusioned and confused. But we'll talk ourselves
down, won't we? "Nobody is perfect," we say. "Nobody gets it right

every time, but no need to be concerned. I can still be right about so many other things, and now I have learned one more fact to add to my arsenal."

You hear the pride dripping from these words. Speaking of cognitive dissonance – how exactly can someone bound to the continual confusion, angst, and anxiety of the fog be so sure of everything? You would think that the daily experience of slogging through the murky, wet mist would put a damper on the arrogance, or that it would temper the instinct to bloviate about all I've learned.

Somehow this humiliating journey failed to bring humility. Instead, it strengthened the inclination to sound more sure of my facts and of myself. In a life bound to insecurity – insecure attachments, feeling less-than, and so often finding relating itself to be harder work – in this life, we counter the negativity by being extra positive somewhere else. We find that diversion to be one of our instincts of survival as members of the Functional Hurting.

As we seek to begin (or continue) the process of rewiring our brains to bring our whole selves to bear on the text of scripture, we have to bring these parts of ourselves with us. The pride, the survival instinct, the obsessive-compulsive need to be right – if that is part of our souls, we have it with us when we read any verse or chapter. We can be tempted to act like church, devotions, and other spiritual disciplines are meant only to make our good parts better, while our bad pieces shrivel and eventually disappear. But in doing so, we censor reactions that would be helpful in applying the text to the whole self. So, let's step into this from that position of pride.

The need to always be right is properly in the category of youth. Teenagers have vexed their parents throughout time by refusing to accept as correct a more nuanced and experienced view of the world. It's a normal stage of development that should be expected. We need it as we grow, because in that stage of life, for the first time, we are putting a lot of different spheres of existence together. So much is unknown, and life gets overwhelming unless we think we understand. And to be fair, at that age, we do have some level of understanding, just not complete.

As our integration of those many spheres becomes more practiced, we're able to add nuance. Many do find ways to grow out of the know-it-all stage in adulthood, as we experience the plethora of things we just don't know. Once we have learned a few times that we were wrong, it should be no surprise to us that we may be wrong again.

Flip the script from normal development, though, and we get a different outcome. Grow up feeling that you are always (or most often) wrong. Perhaps it is the experience of older siblings constantly correcting you to the point of humiliation. Maybe you knew things that the adults around you cared about, but couldn't for the life of you find common ground with your peers. Or, you were right about a lot of things, but you were put down as a person anyway. Trauma will also shake the foundations of the developing mind, calling into question any firm facts and memories.

However it happened, you grew up feeling shame for being less-than: you didn't know what you needed to know, when you needed to know it. From there, you have a lot more work to do to be right for the right reasons.

You see, those of us who feel less-than are searching for power, so we can reverse roles between the haves and the have-nots. Having a certain level of intellect turns into a practical reality that knowledge is power, which seems like the perfect escape from the cage of shame. I know more now, and I know better, so I can leave the cage. More knowledge means more power, meaning that I can always have a leg up on any discussion – I won't have to feel wrongness again.

I can, because I know how. I can get into a conversation, because I've planned out all the ways that talk can go. I can go to the store, because I've thought through where everything is, and I won't look dumb trying to find something right in front of me. I can make this phone call, because I know exactly what to say and won't waste someone's valuable time. These activities become transactional, rather than relational, because they need to be measurable to sustain the belief that I am winning.

But when I am wrong again, as inevitably I will be, my defense of myself breaks down, and I am everything I feared I would be. The conversation takes a different turn than I anticipated. I messed up at the store, or they rearranged the shelves. The phone call didn't turn out the right way. My psyche snaps back into that shameful cage; I am almost nauseated in my disillusionment. And yet, so often I double down on the strategy of just being right the next time.

I'll follow fallacy after fallacy in a pattern of arrested development, because being wrong just once in a while has become a mortal sin condemning me to a life of deserved shame and abasement. In my shame, I'll act like I'm right even when I know I am wrong, because it is easier to offload that wrongness onto someone whom I think can handle it better than I can. It's cheating, but it's unfortunately true.

When this is your pattern, when your self-worth stands on the knife's edge and easily falls into the void on either side, it is a small wonder that being right about God and Jesus has a special charge to it. Even when you take a step in development and start admitting that you may be wrong about some small things – at least you still have this eternal life stuff figured out.

That's what really matters, after all, and you can hang the hat of your psyche right there for it to have a firm foundation. So, I'd better know everything I possibly can in the Bible, and I had best be good at praying too. Something – anything – for when my mind folds in on itself and begins to fall apart in the anxiety and strain – I can say, "At least I have that!"

Picture, then, when someone shows you a verse you've never seen before, that seems to call into question everything that you've put into a nice little doctrinal box tied up with a bow. And you feel that tearing in the soul again – the sorrow as your spirit weeps once more for losing its foundation. It takes time – weeks, perhaps months – and you get back to it. The idea of being right is more important than actually being right. So, you put the bow back on the box, brush it off, and try to forget this happened.

Okay, so you were wrong once, and so was I. Let's go to church to learn, and even to Sunday school. Then we find out we've been wrong again. Let's go to Bible study. Let's go to Bible college. Let's go to the seminary, and learn how to be right about God. Well, first we have to pick the right church or school, because there are different teachings at each one, and no doctrine is insignificant... Let's get our Master of Divinity. It's not enough – we need a doctoral degree now.

Everything I don't know becomes a reminder of the basic life concepts and activities I can't seem to get right. All of this knowledge, and I still don't know how to effectively relate with people. All of these facts, and they don't solve my prayer life. All of that work, all of that pursuit in the name of knowing enough to not feel like a failure.

And how did I get here? Well, by thinking that the search for truth would be fulfilled if I gained insight and saw the signs. All of the things I just naturally don't get, that drag me down in this life, that make me feel shame so deep that I cannot just turn it off: I thought I could solve them all if I just understood a little more.

Where do I go to get that insight? Look for the right signs. How do I know which signs to follow? Well, now, I need more insight. Around and around I go, trying to piece together this complex life – trying to cobble together something that looks like a functional person on this insecure and shifting foundation. I have a lot riding on this, after all. Figuring things out seems to be the one thing I am good at, so I have to project that ever stronger to compensate for (or distract from) all the weakness.

I take that skill that comes most naturally to me, and make it both my way of interacting with the world and my defense from the world. It allows me to function, and I rely on it to keep me from getting hurt. But is it working? Is my experience of God better for knowing all of this stuff? No – more knowing brings more questions and fewer answers.

The words of Paul we consider here may bring some of this into focus. He speaks of Jews and Greeks – in his time, this was essentially a description of his known world and the major groups of people he interacted with on a regular basis. Paul acknowledged that these vastly disparate cultures appealed to different signals to show the way for life.

Those from one culture thought that if there were more miracles, signs, and wonders, that would provide a more sound base for life and faith. Or, on the other side, if there were just greater insight to be had, a more practiced knowledge and its application in life and logic, then the firm foundation would be there. If you have a problem in life, a plateau you just can't push past, you should just need one of those things: a sign to give you direction, or more insight.

Living life by those two principles is most often the path of least resistance, and that's not a bad thing. It would be wrong to ignore the signs in front of us or to eschew the wisdom available for living. But what the author is examining here is that need to assign God a place in our hierarchy of being right. It's that more basic assumption that we know how God works, where to find him, and how he will give direction to his children in this life. We're expecting that he'll give us signs for what we should do, or that more insight will break us out of this fog that we've been in for so long.

We get so twisted up in looking for the signs, we become certain that we've missed them. If only we'd had the wisdom to see them right in front of us! We tie ourselves in knots trying to figure out that last bit of insight we need to bring all of our pain to a head, have it done with, and get on with a more full life. We get stuck there, though, because it is all turned inward – we're looking in a mirror, trying to find the right signs and wisdom to cover over the wounds we see on our faces. We're using the signs and wisdom we find as tools to improve our brand, to fix the projection of ourselves that has failed us so often in the past.

But our need to be right in all these things goes beyond just being able to function in this life. Some driving force deep within us dreams big and wants to change the world. We struggle, because we can barely tolerate the experience of ourselves – and yet, the world needs (we think) to tolerate us for its own good. We see the world in a particular light, we see its wrongs, and we want to fix it.

The search for significance is compelling: we want our lives to have counted for something more than a daily journey of fighting through the wounds of our own souls. A part of us would gladly abandon ourselves as a lost cause, if we could just be that significant influence to make the world a better place. We want to be bright signs showing that we are worth something. In any way we can, we want to provide wisdom to prevent people from following down the same foggy paths that we've walked for so long.

Here again we see the desire for that breakthrough moment – that reaching of catharsis. If we just had that experience, where suddenly our pain up to that moment was plainly worth it... After all, if we were writing the story, that's how we'd set it up. We've grown up with stories that resolve at the end, where the various pains and poignant moments pay off at long last.

It is incredibly frustrating to live a fog experience where that resolution doesn't happen. Instead of being a bright star, we end up being a bit actor in a B-movie – and our career is going nowhere. We have to continue day by day, doing the best we can with what we can see.

The voices we keep hearing are constantly telling us that we have to make something of ourselves. That ours is the generation that will bring great revival to the world. That we should step out into God's plan for our lives, rather than continue to struggle with our thoughts and feelings on a daily basis. That if we would just read our Bibles more and pray more, God would bless us. All of these voices continue to enforce their will, that we would be signs of truth in the world and significant followers of Jesus.

And it is true – one of my most fundamental fears is that I will be seen for what I am: a second-class, useless Christian. That the reason that God isn't doing powerful things in my life is because I'm doing something wrong. The power I desperately seek is to be able to escape from that fear and from that reality. With rocks in our hands, we gather in dark, eager anticipation around someone or some cause. Let me be in the position of power to throw the first stone! It may not matter what the target is; there are so many causes to get behind in this world. Anything but to be the target!

I was thinking recently of the words of Jesus: "He who is without sin, cast the first stone."[24] The Pharisees were smart – they dropped their weapons and walked away. I stayed with the image for a while in my mind, trying to picture how I would act in that situation. And my instinct? Haul back and throw that stone, as hard as I can. The Pharisees chickened out – I'll show them! Peter, likewise, was not so smart when he got the chance. In the garden, as soldiers came to take Jesus away, he raised his weapon to be the first to lash out.[25] Jesus reprimanded him. In his situation, honestly, I would probably cower in the shadows, but Jesus wouldn't have approved of that either.

My fear of the pain of being what I am drives me to act in ways that seem righteous to some, but are actually calculated defense mechanisms. If I stay quiet and fly under the radar, I won't attract the attention of those who would defend their turf by throwing stones. If I make sure that I am right, then when I sense danger near, I can rise up to throw the first stone and distract from any weakness in my position. That is why I will go to many lengths to be right, or as a close second, to be seen as the person who is right.

The pressure mounts, though, because "they" want to see the results now. You know who they are – they seem nice, but you feel drained after interacting with them. They bring expectations that we can't reach, and problems that we can't solve. They're not waiting for a process, for us to resolve some of the things going on between God and us. They're not making allowances for our broken relational hardware, our struggle to see the real, or our tumultuous encounters with the blazing figure in the fog. Those who are looking for validation for their own search for significance will burn what little fuel we have, wittingly or not.

But we need to hear something: it is OK to fail in that enterprise. If we have walked in the fog, if we have struggled to function in everyday life (let alone the faith), it is alright to give ourselves permission to attend to the needs of our souls. That one extra insight won't solve everything, but we may find bits of relief if we starve the significance monster. Those are some of the words the figure in fire speaks to us in the fog. He repeats them again, and again – we begin to hear them as we become still from exhaustion, as we realize that making ourselves signs and wonders is more work than we can bear.

He himself is the sign for peace and truth. He showed the world he is worth something, and he shows us where the truth is. Jesus' death is the sign that we escape God's wrath. He broke the bonds of death as a sign that we may also escape the cold fingers of the fog. And Jesus is the wisdom. He points to life lived before God, waiting on God, watching for God. He shows us a paradigm of a life based on grace.

Jesus is the truth we are searching for, and he is also the significance we seek. And his significance is not just self-fulfilling to validate himself: he shares that significance with any who will follow him.

He did abandon himself, and he did bear momentous influence in turning the world on its edge.

So, it sounds like the fog would dispel if we just add Jesus, right? Many of us have tried this simple adjustment, and launched ourselves into the effort so valiantly that we would look down on the "common" Christian. I am not proud of this, but it is true: having abandoned my ability to make myself a sign, I took hold of Jesus, only to treat him as a launching pad to make myself a sign once more.

I can use Jesus as one more way to gain the whole world, to make myself significant. We are so focused on the resolution of the tension that we skip all kinds of steps to get there. We deeply want that to be the way it works, that we give the fog to Jesus and he just brightens our day.

Our walk in the fog isn't like that, though, is it? And that's why we keep on walking away for a while, because we're angry. Angry that we pray daily through a litany of thoughts that try to stop us. Mad that at long last, we still don't hear God's voice as others do. Frustrated that reading the Bible doesn't make us hear the angels sing. So, we stay in a cycle of coming to the end of ourselves, hearing the voice of our true Hope once more, then again using him as the step up we need to be the sign we want to be.

No, the blazing figure doesn't make the fog go away rapidly. But he says, "We met here in the fog. I will be with you in the fog for as long as you journey here, because I won't leave you or abandon you." If there's one thing for us to do differently, it is this: stop trying so hard to make ourselves shine so brightly. Jesus would have us remember, even if we don't realize, that he is with us in the fog. We don't need to prove ourselves or spend our lives in the service of validating how other people experience him. He calls us to a simpler existence.

He understands our weakness, and he is not threatened by our lack of vision. He is not walking away.

The foolishness of God is wiser than men, and the weakness of God is stronger than men.

1 Corinthians 1:25

13. Redemption

I am sure of this, that he who began a good work in you will bring it to completion at the day of Jesus Christ.

Philippians 1:6

There are a couple of ways I can be a hypocrite in the eyes of the world. The first kind is pretty obvious: sin with reckless abandon, and then pretend to be all pious at church on Sunday. I can put on airs that I'm an exemplary Christian but just be constantly calculating what I can get away with. I'd keep my sin relatively hidden but have no particular shame over it. I wouldn't want to be caught, because I'd have too much to lose: I want to be seen as a good person.

The world would see my lack of internal consistency in the Christian life and rightly look down on me for it. Granted, a Christian's behavior should not be (and is not) defined by the world – for those principles, we ought to look to scripture. But the way that some Christians have acted over the centuries has brought harm to the reputation of Christ and the church. The world is often more cognizant of the disparity than is the church itself.

There is more than one way to be a pretender, though. The obvious hypocrite assumes he is okay and just has to hide some of his sin to stay okay. On the other hand, a more subtle actor is fully aware that she is a wretched sinner in need of grace – but needs to hide weakness and deficiency to be accepted. In other words, I know my sin all too well, and I know Jesus has brought me back to God. But I feel the need to daily curry favor with God and others by bringing greater worthiness to the table.

For Christ-followers like this, we end up trying way too hard because we have something to prove. We want to be known as Christians, but there is an insecurity there in which we despair that nobody likes us – including God. We want very much to be appreciated, but we don't feel like we fit in very naturally. So, we push the angle of being good or exemplary Christians because we feel like that is the silver bullet – the one thing that will get us over the threshold of belonging.

We understand we still sin daily but continually try to function as though sin damage has no influence over our personhood and relationships anymore. Having that damage would harm our chances of staying in the group. When people look down on us or don't like us, we can look around and try our best to build a coalition around ourselves: "Can you believe they don't like us? We're Christians, and we haven't hurt them! ... you still like us, right?"

There is a lack of internal consistency for this set of Christians, too: one that projects a front of "Christ is my strength, whom shall I fear" but functions in an insecure, fearful manner. And the world calls them hypocrites, too, but that's wrong: the true hypocrites hide their sin, but these others conceal their pain and wounds.

We know these souls more properly as the Functional Hurting, dwellers in the fog. We who are aware of the fog are wary of our tendencies to stand up and proclaim that all is well in our souls, when we know the opposite is true. It's not a lie, we think, but a declaration of faith...

The yearning in our souls for inward peace is so great that we will often jump to fake it until we make it – trying to speak it into being. Those who are in the fog, but (as yet) unaware of it, subconsciously do the same. The world calls them "hypocrites" because they correctly ascertain the inauthenticity – a self-splitting denial that has them operating, as it were, as half-people. We intimately know that insecurity and how much it colors everything we do, think, and feel.

We in the fog are afraid of God. That's not something that comes to us primarily from the Bible – we are much more driven by the broken God-image built into our neural networks. We can understand and accept the gospel, that through Jesus' death and resurrection we may trade our sins for his righteousness, and on that basis, we have an objective status of peace with God.

But the God-image built into us by parental figures, various authorities, and teachers does not let us off the hook. Our continued lack of feeling peace is, in itself, a condemnation to our daily lives, and we expect wrath. We are so engrained with this version of functional deity that it colors all of our considerations of life and the world around us.

We have anxious attachments to God, and so an insecure relationship. Even after Jesus, then, we still function as though we have to be the best version of ourselves to have God's favor in our lives. There is a part of me that still believes I can do that – "It can't be so hard," I say, "to set aside sinful attitudes and say no to things that keep me away from God." I still want that storybook Christian life, after all, where God did great things through me because I got my life right.

Eventually, I've tired of the constant fight against all of the distractions from that great life, whether sin or weakness. Then, I'm left with one certain message from my insecurity: I'm just not good enough to continue. In fake-it-till-you-make-it world, I need to take action. I need to subtract the pieces of myself that are keeping me from arriving.

So, I start doing spiritual surgery on myself: trying to slice off the inner angst I suffer. Trying to take out the inner voice that I assume is the "flesh." Trying to stave off the cognitive dissonance related to my God-image, my concept of who God is and how he functions among us.

On the one hand, there is something there that feels noble, like a good work or sacrifice that will bring good results. After all, if we allow our struggle and flesh a voice, surely others may be led in a similar path of sin, right? When we get to the point of feeling this way, though, we have allowed some dissonances to cloud into the fog around us.

First, we have taken a position of weakness, one in which we cannot seem to make headway in the Christian life, and recast it as noble strength (aka martyrdom). In my weakness, I have to do serious work on my weakness to stop it from being a powerful force in the lives of others. Or, I believe that by using my weakness to take away the unmentionable parts of my soul, I somehow become stronger.

Worse, though, is that we are taking great strides to reconcile with an image of God in our neural networks that is capricious, easily offended, and quickly angered. Ideally, we would reform this internal representation of the divine, in order to have at least a closer approximation of relationship with his true person. Instead of healing that inner concept of God, though, we spend our time and our energy trying to find a way to keep the broken one that is there from judging us.

There is psychological danger here: in our addled, ill-informed, and often debilitated state, we are cutting into the fabric of our own psyches and souls. We're trying to shape ourselves to impress someone. We're not getting the feedback we really want from the God-image within us – in fact, what we're hearing is a near-constant stream of negativity. The voices around us that resonate are likewise the negative ones, because they remind us of a very familiar feeling.

Deep down, though, we know that such existence is unsustainable, and we must take steps to change it. Getting validation is so important in our anxious attachment patterns, then, that we will trade the integrity of our own souls to get it. Often, we take a wounded soul and simply wound it more.

And that is what we're trying to avoid, so desperately: the experience of being wounded souls. We are so afraid of getting alone with our selves and with our thoughts, because we know what darkness lurks there. Our anxiety drives us to live louder on the outside, to try to project a reality about ourselves, and hope against hope that it will eventually permeate our inner beings.

We think we can make our insides match up to what we've projected. But then we've made the inside hurt worse – not only for being deficient, but also for being crushed through the machinations of attempts to make it better. We follow the cycle to make the outside even better. "Perhaps," I begin to think, "if my inner being is always going to lag behind my projected goodness, I just need to make the projection very much better, so my inner being will rise to an acceptable level!" Instead, we make the divide greater, then rinse and repeat until we drop from the strain.

This anxious approach to God and relationships also spills over into community dynamics. If our concept of Christians is that they're supposed to be the "good" people, who do "good" things, then I'll feel the need to be as good as I can possibly be. From my position of inner insecurity, I have a need to be better than all the other people, so I can have my behavior validated by the good people around me. My behavior will also validate theirs, which feels good to them – but with my weak emotional boundaries, I feel some of that satisfaction as my own.

Being good in such a community is supposed to make Jesus more palatable to people around me. If only those outside the group could see how good he made me! And if they knew how good they really want to be (in their heart of hearts), they'd know they need him! It's the way I'm supposed to "win" at life: I've got it made if I can look at those around me and defend the idea that I'm better at the whole Jesus thing than they are.

And that's not saying I deserve his salvation – of course not. Instead, it is a question of how I can function to finally feel validation from the broken God-image in my neural networks. The type of community we've described here would seem to be one that promotes functional piety among many. But for those in the fog, it will often turn into a communal version of the same soul-surgery: cut out the ones who aren't keeping up, and fear being cut out yourself. This paradigm is how we naturally think, feel, and behave when our God-image is damaged in this way.

After all, if we were fully integrated and relating properly, we would be loving God and others in freedom, without the existential anxiety. What we're left with, though, is living out a constant set of manipulations designed to bring people and God into line with the way I want life to work. We do much of this subconsciously, as we naturally seek out that validation and gravitate toward it.

The signal flare that our souls send up for notice is the massive amount of energy draining from us, simply to achieve or maintain some equilibrium. We have tried to be the exemplary ones. Instead, we found ourselves running on empty just trying to do the simple things. It seems unfair, doesn't it, that the added effort did not yield more fruitful results.

Coming from a place of believing that Christians are better than other people (and better at life), it can be hard to imagine that someone outside the faith may have a healthier mind, system of emotions, and relationships than I do. After all, I'm saved, and they're not – shouldn't I be in better psychological condition by default?

I wish that were the case! But when dealing with particular challenges, or living with mental illness, or recovering from certain traumas, that baseline assumption is implausible. A great deal more energy is required to function "normally," and we may have trouble noticing when our thought patterns and emotions start to go awry.

When I was growing up, my family would take trips to my grandparents' house in Indiana. That house was very old, and it had settled in a lot of places. Most of the doors wouldn't shut properly anymore – and those that did, wouldn't stay shut by themselves. When I say settled, though... The kitchen was in the back and noticeably sloped down toward the back of the house. And there was a bedroom that slanted even more toward the back corner. Any time I walked into those rooms, there was always a particular instant of my brain having to snap to that new coordinate grid from normal, because the room was out of sync with the rest of the plane of my existence.

Living with psychological challenges and mental illness, no matter how mild or severe, can be like living in a house where the floor tilts. There can be vast areas of life that seem normal, and then we walk through that one door and boom! We're leaning to the left. So, we get used to the idea that the floor isn't straight, for whatever reason. We train ourselves to handle it sloping in a certain direction – make ourselves lean the other way so the door looks straight.

It gets tricky in real life, though – next day, we wake up, lean the way we learned, and just fall right on over. After we pick ourselves up and dust ourselves off, we see that we fell because the floor now tilts the other way instead. Great – now we have to relearn the basics, and apparently, they can change at any time.

So, it takes a lot more energy to accommodate the necessary heightened awareness, continually set up and reset coping mechanisms, and just keep standing up. That's not even considering what energy it would take to determine what structural weakness led to this severity of tilting in the floor – or what it will take to make it better.

Perhaps it is true that as Christians follow Jesus, they should trend toward sinning less and less. But the psyche and the soul do not instantly heal and become properly meshed together at the point of trusting Jesus. We can't put all of our eggs in the one basket of that past salvation – so much in our lives is still broken. It is strange that though we often go through deep psychological and emotional pain, we still tell ourselves it's all supposed to be alright already, because Jesus. Eventually, it will be, for sure. Just not yet. There remains a dissonance, and so there remains a further need for salvation.

In some manner, we Christ-followers in the fog are existing like Old Testament saints. Of course, we do know how God's plan of salvation unfolds in Jesus, and we have a certain clarity of how that should affect life. And we do have the Holy Spirit. But due to our damaged creation existence, there are present benefits of trusting in Jesus that we are not experiencing. So, we have to look to the future, just as they did in times of old. It feels as though our faith has to be much stronger in the unseen, because we do not see.

In the present, though, we fear the figure in flame, who we again and again encounter in the fog. Our dissonant concept of him drives us to solve that remaining salvation for ourselves. We walk away from him again and again, acknowledging his future benefit but refusing his grace for present daily life.

To be sure, not everyone in our position tries harder. For some of us, as we await that future, final salvation, we go so far as to fill the interim by escape. Especially now that we live in an age of easy entertainment, we will gladly spend days of our lives watching how other people have spent days of their lives. We allow others to make the choices, take the risks, bear the consequences, and reap the rewards – all while putting more of our own lives in the rear-view mirror.

We see our own existence as a way of pain, of daily tension and often confusion. An over-reliance on the power of story brings a separation for us – one that matches our weaker boundaries. We blur the line that separates us from other people and that divides their emotions from our own. In so doing, we attain fuller identification with the stories we are reading and watching.

Certainly, there is nothing wrong with using entertainment and engaging the imagination in stories. With the possibility of binge-watching in modern culture, though, we have the opportunity to stay in pursuits as a full substitute for existence. For those with enmeshed patterns, there is much less risk to allow a canned story and characters to trespass our boundaries, than to allow living, more volatile people the same access.

Stories do not have expectations for us, but people do. Stories do not involve interaction, but people certainly do. With that lesser risk, though, we surrender any reward we would gain by taking the life we have in front of us and working through our own story.

Even in the fog, though, some of us do muster up the energy to do something other than escape or avoidance. These efforts may come in fits and spurts, but they do happen – usually when we've tired of our current walk away from the blazing figure and have decided it's high time we get our act together (again). We can have an idea of what the "good Christian" looks like, and we'll plot a course to get there.

We know it won't be an overnight transformation, and there are those pesky emotions to deal with that we can't seem to turn off and on. But we'll have our set of activities that we need to do – the program to follow. Surely, we think, if we can line up our efforts with the prescribed methods, perhaps we'll get a glimpse of those temporal benefits of salvation that we want to experience.

Sometimes we pick a guru to help us out or lead us, someone we think is cool and has it together – or someone we just want to like us. We'll follow them for a while, until we understand that they are just as fallen as we are. And then we can either abandon the program for a while, or we can double down and find the next best person to follow. Remember, the fog has many twists and turns, and the mists will obscure enough of a person (at first) to fool us into thinking they are the one to follow.

When we do this exercise of picking a suitable sage, though, we often minimize our own experiences, learned lessons, and known weaknesses. Often, these fellow Christ-followers have not gone through large parts of our stories. They're not dealing with the same sorts of trials, temptations, and neural networks.

As we ante up our escape mechanisms and growth-seeking programs for ourselves, we are again following the principle that though Jesus has saved us, we still need to invent the best version of ourselves. As a stance toward the blazing figure we encounter in the fog, we have brought our damaged souls fully to bear against the savior: we raise ourselves up as finishers of what God started. I needed Jesus for the sin and wrath of God thing, but the rest of this I treat more as a puzzle: if I just put the pieces together in the right order, I'll be fine.

In our frenzy to piece ourselves back together, though, what we miss is that we were never masters of our own creation. We didn't make ourselves whole to begin with, then get broken, and now must reconstruct who we know ourselves to be. In the fog, we really want to be the overcomers. We want to snap out of that confusion and learn that one weird trick that opens up the path to a satisfying walk with Jesus.

But in the fall of mankind and our own personal failings, the beings we were created to be have been damaged in more ways than we can possibly understand or imagine. We have experienced traumas of the soul and of the mind, and we do not innately have the necessary wisdom or power to reverse that. We don't contain the complete picture.

Each of our lives is like a beautiful and valuable vase that has been broken with sin, damage, trauma, and the resulting psyche. What happens to the vase when God saves us through Jesus? With the mists of the fog swirling around and confusing us, it feels as though God put all of the pieces back together, and then said, "Now don't break it again!" But of course, I did, and now I have to figure out how to fix it before I am found out.

Now, if it really worked that way, I'd have a problem: I don't know what the completed vase looks like. It's not like a store-bought jigsaw puzzle, where I'd at least have the picture on the box. I just have these shards of pottery. Some of them are sharp, and they cut me when I'm trying to fit things together. I drop some of the other pieces, and they shatter into smaller bits.

Thankfully, life does not work that way. God did not put all the pieces back together at the point of salvation, and he does not expect us to put ourselves back together again. We are in a fog that, while opaque and mysterious to us, is plain and clear to him.

He has the final picture, he has the wisdom and power necessary, and he says he will get us there. He began the process, and he will finish it. Jesus is the savior. That's what he does. That's his job. And, according to the Bible, it's what he wants to do.

Knowing this fact does not instantly cure us from the fog that pervades our neural networks and souls. Grasping this concept will not be a shortcut to abundant life or a fast track to rocking Christianity. What it does give us, though, is our one escape that won't have us wasting our lives. We get one thing to tell ourselves when we feel like our house of cards is falling to the ground.

When we are reading our Bibles and we can't figure out what God is telling us, relax: God knows what it is, and God will finish his work in us.

When we wake up in the morning and find that the floor has tilted on us again, we need to hear that God does not expect us to put ourselves back together. He knows our pain and disorientation, and he will bring us to the finish line.

When we are clinically depressed, and we're having trouble finding the energy and motivation to get up and do life for a while, we need to hear that God will finish what he started. It doesn't mean we'll stop feeling down, or that the functions of life will magically come together. But it does mean that our lives are making progress even when we don't have the strength.

When we feel the paralysis of an anxiety that is springing from deeply-set traumatic experiences and soul wounds, we need to hear that Jesus will walk with us in those parts of the fog too. Knowing the savior in the garden of Gethsemane will not likely make the fear go away. But it will speak truth into our souls, even if we do not feel that assurance, that God is working within us and will finish what he started.

When we finally wake up from a long bout with addiction, and we don't know what to do first, hear the message: God wants us to be whole, but God doesn't expect us to know how to do that right away. He is still at work in us. We may not even know the true extent of the damage we have experienced in our souls, but he will bring us to the goal.

The point is not that our experience is irrelevant, or that our efforts are entirely wasted. Our daily lives are meaningful even in the struggle. What the blazing figure in the fog is telling us, and what draws us to come back to him again and again, is that he wants to accompany us on our journey. Our experience and efforts are just part of the grace that he allows in our lives. His daily presence is a much larger grace – one that he would have us embrace even if we don't have a tangible experience from it.

Our efforts will be freed from the pressure of putting ourselves back together and making signs and wonders of ourselves. Our experiences will be freed of the weight of needing to be make-or-break lessons that would have brought us to the mountaintops of Christian spiritual existence. We may be left in a position of rest, even though our fog-filled souls feel only the edge of it.

Listen to the figure in flame when you find him in the fog. He whispers words of peace and rest, calling you to draw your hands down from your face, so his light will touch and heal the wounds and flesh. He says, "I know you can't see your way very well, and that you can't hear my voice very well. But I will stay with you in the places you don't know, and I will keep speaking my love so you will hear me when you can. I want to bring you somewhere better, where all the air is clear, and all the sounds are crisp. It will take us a while to get there. I know that you are hurting in ways you understand – and in ways you aren't aware of yet. But I have overcome pain larger than the universe itself.

"I am a savior – that's what I do. I will put the pieces back together for you, and in time, I will give you lasting rest. Let's walk through the fog together."

Christ also, having been offered once to bear the sins of many, will appear a second time for salvation without reference to sin, to those who eagerly await Him.

Hebrews 9:28

14. Relief

He will not cry out or raise His voice,
Nor make His voice heard in the street.

A bruised reed He will not break
And a dimly burning wick He will not extinguish;
He will faithfully bring forth justice.

Isaiah 42:2-3

To live in our world is to experience pressure. Pressure can be good. We get it almost from the moment we are born – the expectation that over time, we will develop that specific set of skills we need to carry through daily life. We start with the basics of eating, sleeping, and moving around, which are essential for most of us. Parenting, community, schooling, friends, and institutions of society propel us toward functional living.

And, of course, pressure can be bad, or at least painful – which has been the subject of this book. Needs are often only partially met by imperfect and broken systems. Our jobs may not be fulfilling, but we feel the load of providing for ourselves and our families. So, we find ways to cope and earn a living. Our skills at relating may not be very good, but we feel the strain of isolating ourselves and avoiding other people. So, we find ways to cope and go out in public. Perhaps we have experienced traumatic events that continue to impress themselves on our consciousness – we feel compression against our psyche, but we do not want to be defined by those imprints. So, we find ways to cope.

The fog we have been exploring throughout this book is a place of pressure all around us. Here, we have the stress of straining our eyes to see, trying to figure out which shapes and movements in the fog are real. We can feel the mass of voices around us – so many, it becomes almost impossible to sort through to find those which would be both true and beneficial. Our taste is so affected by our wounds that we often gravitate toward modes of existence that are not good for us – like escape, addiction, and isolation.

And then we have that way of relating with God, or rather the picture of God built into our neural networks. Our effort doesn't end up with abundant life and fullness of joy. In fact, when we encounter God in the fog, our gut reaction is shame rooted in fear.

So many burdens we have to lay at the feet of the only one who can contain them! But we fear, because even if God is on our side, he may take hold of us so firmly and with such strength that we will break right in half. We feel the weight of glory: it is as though we are lying face down before him, and the pressure of him comes down as a knee to the spine.

Melancholy, depression, and anxiety have always been notable conditions. The fog is nothing new. Perhaps it is more widespread today. Or, possibly, greater evaluation and statistics have brought a much greater awareness of these conditions to society as a whole.

Getting clarity on how we spend our lives and the way that impacts our mental health is difficult. Hindsight can be 20-20. But present cloudiness and anxiety from the future can cloud our perception of the past. In the moment, we have little clear vision to evaluate.

The fog's magnitude is quite poignant when discussing it in spiritual terms, but that's not to say it necessarily has a spiritual cause (aside from the general fallen state of the universe). The fog's specific origins for each of us can remain shrouded in mystery. But with practice, we can find threads and patterns in our lives that have given the fog additional substance.

Navigating the fog can be a survival skill, worthy of the time and energy it takes to observe cause and effect. We constantly evaluate our energy levels and how much pressure we can take from any one vector. Let's consider a few of the circumstances that, for many of us, will naturally deepen the mist.

First: work. Many of us are entrenched for years and decades in jobs. We trade time, i.e. pieces of our lives, for money. Without these jobs, we don't eat, but within them, we don't feel alive. We are under pressure to be efficient and productive above most other considerations, and we have no idea how that will affect our neural networks over time.

Survival is a strong instinct here – if we don't make our work profitable for the company, our jobs are in jeopardy. So, we can psychologically split to fulfill that survival, rather than integrating each experience. We need to constantly tell ourselves, "I can feel that thing (frustration, anxiety, fatigue, what have you) later. For now, I need to let it go, or at least set it aside, so I can do my job properly."

How well and how long that holds up will depend on each person. Generally speaking, though, training yourself to compartmentalize your being during significant portions of your existence will lead to stunted development in the underused portions. That affects our abilities to relate with others, to deal with adverse emotions, and to build and realize hopes and dreams.

Next: information, now ever-present and available at our fingertips. While we gain extensive benefits from our massive store of data, with that advancement we have lost some element of process. We no longer need to puzzle through concepts and problems – we can simply find someone who has done so before and get the summary. In fact, we have built on this worldwide library for long enough that we'll find people who have compared and contrasted several solutions to a problem, so we can pick and choose, still without the exercise of process.

More troubling is the idea that we have lost the ability to live with ambiguity – we have practiced instant gratification for a very long time, and it is difficult to exist in that space of knowing I have a question but not having the answer. Many works have been written in lament of the transformation of the human into the extension of machine. The person loses intrinsic value in favor of serving the collective information store.

A third pressure is the one that binds the human-nodes in that information collective together. Communication is constant: phone calls, text messages, emails, the 24/7 news cycle, and all the social media in between. In times past, we had a little more control over how we presented our demeanor and ideas. Now, moment to moment, precious little separation remains between our instantaneous thoughts and the image of ourselves that we project toward the world.

What we put out there for consumption gets judged promptly and aggressively for IQ, callousness, and lack of accepted morality or willpower. Are we efficient and effective members of this human collective? Or do we have the same insecure foundations and fears toward humanity that we've discovered in the church?

We have to keep all of the plates of our thoughts and positions spinning and also do concurrent PR management! Some may say, "If you can't take the heat, get out of the kitchen!" But even if we avoid presenting ourselves on social media at all, we can still feel the weight of expectation upon us, because being silent is judged as well.

For those of us with boundary weaknesses (such as many or most of us in the fog), all of these processes are extraordinarily intrusive. Perhaps boundary issues are more prevalent now than they were historically. Or, the stakes are much higher in today's mode of communication, which makes those weaknesses of greater importance.

Each of the spheres above brings pressure that could break us, but let's dig deeper for one more. The avenues of entertainment that we have now are far more prevalent than they were, even compared to a quarter century ago. We can go on constant tangents while in the fog – all without taking any time to promote our awareness of who we are, where we are, and how this truth affects our life experience. What's more, the sheer number of options can give us decision paralysis. Ironic, isn't it – we feel a pressure to maximize the efficiency even of our entertainment, which was supposed to be a relief from the other facets of life that demand such productivity.

The fog we are in comes from foundational, relational building blocks of our psyche being out of sync. We have the external pressures and effects of society, family, and faith. Then, we have the internal pressures and effects of mental health, life experience, and personal decisions. Like tectonic plates rubbing against each other, some of these cut sharper than others and wound our souls.

These pressures roam around our minds and hearts, poking and prodding at various points until they find a weak spot to break through. They quench our motivation and make us feel tired, which leads to dysfunctional behavior and sinful choices, which leads to more weak spots, and so it goes.

We are the bruised and bent reeds. We, the Functional Hurting, are the candles that are smoking without flame. The pressures of this world will break us in pieces. The forces, voices, and constant choices this world provides will put out that last hint of fire in our lives and leave us cold in the dark. Despite the strength we think we have, the least miscalculation will leave us crushed.

Contrast that with the picture given of our savior, Jesus, the blazing figure in the fog: though he is powerful, he does not break us. Though he is like a mighty wind in the force he can bring, he does not snuff us out. We struggle to communicate and relate, but he will not press to the point of breaking us apart. He will not crush us by stepping on our past traumas and current anxieties.

Remember the people of Israel who were exiled to a foreign land? The exile meant they could not experience the benefits of the land God had placed them in: the promised land. These were bruised people, bent over in grief as the foundations of their daily life were swept away.

Many of the exiled would die in captivity and never see their homeland again. But God had not given up on his promises. Instead, the goal posts were moved farther out, so that much more had to happen and be orchestrated by God to bring the promise to fulfillment.

We who live with the experience of exile may rest assured: life abundant and fullness of joy will be ours! God apparently isn't waving a magic soul-healing wand over us right now, but he's not giving up on his promises either. He is not fazed by our broken relational hardware, or our traumatic experiences, or our addictions. Our problems may not be solved fully in this lifetime. But through faith and patience, we will inherit the promises.

And so, we will end with a little perspective. I have deliberately avoided presenting quick solutions to the fog throughout this book. Perhaps there are some out there, but that's hardly the point – every one of us is different, and there will be no "silver bullet."

The damage our created selves have experienced isn't wiped out by just adding a little Jesus to the mix. We don't just flip a switch to make the fog go away. It won't dispel if we would just employ that "one weird trick." So how do we move forward? Well, since a great many of the pressures we experience seek to generate chaos, simplifying is key.

The power of a supportive spouse, family, group of friends, and church cannot be overstated. In a world with so many voices, having a healthy few whom we can trust is invaluable. Trained counselors are practiced in the art of active listening; they can help us gain perspective where we've had blind spots.

Companions, friends, and counselors are a safe space for us to learn to express our true selves – our valuable yet wounded selves. They can help us find balance among the chaos, and they give us a place to focus on someone else through listening to and interacting with their stories. In relationship, we can drop some of our survival-related filters that counterintuitively prevent parts of us from growing.

In finding balance, we will do well to allow each part of our lives to serve its own function. When we burden various facets of existence with additional duties, they begin to fail us. For example, theology: knowing the attributes and character of God is very important for us to know what trust we may place in his promises. And there is a great deal of wisdom to be applied throughout life through the imitation of Jesus.

But if we saddle theology up with needing to solve our emotional and relational difficulties, it will fail. Our problem is not that we're not Calvinist enough, or Lutheran enough, etc. We can have theology that is so tight our shoes squeak, but it will fail us if we think it is the means to fix our relational hardware. Truth is truth, but as we've talked about, it doesn't necessarily change subjective experience. Never become codependent with your theology.

When we let each life-piece have its place, that frees us to relax a bit into the grace that is there for us. We're not solving a puzzle made up of our sins, memories, hopes, and dreams. We're not going to "level up" by fitting them all together.

No – continuing in the Christian walk is simply grace to us. We may not (and often don't) see how God is moving us toward completion, but we don't have to. We may not know how God is molding our thoughts and psyches through exposure to his words. But we don't have to.

What we have, always, is the present moment. What we have is knowing that God has continued to work in and through us. We have exposure to his word that is changing our souls. His character persists, even as a person who remains mysterious to us in our fogged vision.

But the simplicity we can find is in knowing that we don't have to try so hard. We didn't land ourselves in the fog, and we don't need to save ourselves from it. The negativity of the experience can be distressing, of course. But we can still look out to the goalposts of the future, see that there will be relief, and then be faithful with what we have each day.

That faithfulness will look different for each one of us, given the various weaknesses and past experiences we have. But there is no such thing as time wasted when walking with Jesus, even in the fog. At the end, I suspect we will find that we understood more of his character and more of his grace than we had ever thought.

Jesus himself remains faithful to the children of God – he is not ashamed to be with us.

No one who is born of God sins, because His seed abides in him; and he cannot sin, because he is born of God.

1 John 1:9

Epilogue

I awake in a sunlit world with ringing ears. Instinctively, I shut my eyes – the light is so bright, and my eyes are accustomed to a darker realm of cold gray. How I got here, I have no idea. I don't recall travelling here, but there is no sign of the fog that surrounded me even as I drifted off to sleep. The light brings with it warming heat – not burning, but a refreshing respite from the dark chill I have inhabited so long.

As I venture to open my eyes – just a slit, at first, then more bravely – I marvel at just how clear my sight is now. Gone is the obscuring cloud. Gone, my inability to see where I'm going, even to look at where I am placing my feet. Gone, my urge to run away and escape a claustrophobic prison of mist. Everything has distinct edges, and I can see where land ends and sky begins.

The ringing in my ears begins to subside after a bit. I become aware that while my eyes start adjusting to the light, my ears are shocked by the lack of noise. Not silence, really – there are sounds, like some birds singing, a gentle breeze, and some conversation off in the distance.

But there are no voices pressing in on me now. No one is telling me what to think, how to feel, and who to believe. I'm suddenly aware that since waking, I haven't heard from my inner critic – the voice that so effectively shamed and defined me for so long. This absence is strange but welcome, like feeling the warm sun after standing in a cold, hard rain.

I lift my hands to my face – now that I am in a place that I can see, maybe I can get a better idea of how bad my wounds are. As I touch, I expect the searing pain from open wounds, the jagged edges of broken skin, and the hardness of old scabs. Instead, I find whole, smooth skin, and I feel no discomfort.

Though incredulous, my touch becomes less ginger. I feel all over my face, head, neck, and arms, only to find none of my old wounds. Even the scars are gone – no pits, creases, or wrinkles. Even the pain itself seems like a distant memory, like I have slept for years before waking here.

Rising up, buoyed by these revelations, I feel steady on my feet on the even ground. Time to venture forth, take a path, and explore this new place. In a way, the path seems familiar to me, as if I had been here before. But it has been so long since I have walked in true sunlight, I don't remember any of it. Walking through the trees, I admire the colors – various hues of green leaves, brown wood, and colorful foliage.

As I come to a clearing in the trees, I find a man waiting. His back is to me at first. Since I am in a place both welcoming and strange, I am a little unsure of myself. I do not call out to him, preferring to wait and observe. Presently, though, he turns toward me, and his face betrays recognition: he knows me. He calls my name, and strides toward me. In the fog, I would have shrunk back from this advance. Here, I step forward.

The fog had been ever-present, borne from a past, and had threatened to consume my future as well. Finally, though, through no action or effort of my own, I have been brought to this pleasant place of light and warmth. As I talk with my friend, I recognize him from his words: he was the mystic blazing figure in the fog. He was the one I had found, then hidden from, then found again so many times. He was the one whose kind words I had spurned. He was the one who spoke words of grace and understanding in a place of demerit and chaos.

Strangely, I feel no residual shame from my prior actions. My friend's words have finally taken root and effect in my mind. No longer am I planning out the conversation with him to try to hedge my bets or cast myself in the best light. Our words flow freely, harmoniously, almost as if we had known each other all my life.

Eventually, I grow brave and ask him where the fog went. He pauses, smiles, puts his hand on my shoulder: "It's gone. Your fog has gone away and will never come back. I'm glad I could walk through it with you for a while, even though it was hard for you to see and hear me. But now you're here, where you belong. A part of you has been here for a long time, but now that you have been called to your reward, you are whole. Here is abundant life and joy. There are many here who have awaited your arrival, and they will be very excited to see you now."

My reluctance to relate and instinct to isolate now gone with their foggy origin, I take my savior's hand and speak clearly: "Let's go meet them!"

Endnotes

All Bible citations unless otherwise indicated: *New American Standard Bible*. La Habra, CA: Foundation Publications, for the Lockman Foundation, 1971. Print.

1. *Fight Club*. Directed by David Fincher, 20th Century Fox, 1999.

2. *Chariots of Fire*. Directed by Hugh Hudson, Warner Bros., 1981. Words written by Colin Welland, and spoken by Eric Liddell's character.

3. Genesis 4:10, *Holy Bible*, New International Version. Zondervan Publishing House, 1984.

4. 2 Thessalonians 2:17, paraphrased.

5. 2 Corinthians 10:5.

6. Philippians 4:8.

7. *Odyssey* XII, 39.

8. Psalm 42:3.

9. Matthew 11:28.

10. John 6:35.

11. John 4:14, NIV.

12. John 10:10.

13. *Mad TV*. Fox, 12 May 2001, disc 140.

14. Wesley, Charles. *And Can It Be*. 1738.

15. Hebrews 11:6.

16. Petty, Tom. *Refugee*. 1979.

17. McLanahan, Sara, et al. "The Causal Effects of Father Absence." *Annual Review of Sociology*, vol. 39, no. 1, 30 July 2013, pp. 399–427, www.ncbi.nlm.nih.gov/pmc/articles/PMC3904543/, 10.1146/annurev-soc-071312-145704.

18. Hudson, Ralph. *At the Cross*. 1885.

19. Miles, C. Austin. *In the Garden*. 1913.

20. Linkin Park. *Somewhere I Belong*. 2003.

21. Jeremiah 39:11-14.

22. Matthew 5:30, *ESV Bible*. Crossway, 2001, www.esv.org/.

23. Miles, C. Austin. *In the Garden*. 1913.

24. John 8:7, paraphrased.

25. John 18:10.

Suggested Reading

Cloud, Henry. *Boundaries Updated and Expanded Edition: When to Say Yes, How to Say No to Take Control of Your Life (Enlarged).* Zondervan, 2017.

Johnson, Eric. *Foundations for Soul Care a Christian Psychology Proposal.* Ivp Academic, 2014.

Nouwen, Henri J M. *Here and Now : Living in the Spirit with Guide for Reflection.* New York, Crossroad, 2003.

Plass, Richard, and James Cofield. *The Relational Soul: Moving from False Self to Deep Connection.* Ivp Books, 2014.

Thrall, Bill, et al. *Truefaced : Trust God and Others with Who You Really Are.* Colorado Springs, Colo., Navpress, 2004.

About the Author

Matt Lewellyn is a husband, foster/adoptive father, and elder in the local church. Having grown up in Connecticut, he now resides outside of Louisville, KY, where he attended seminary. After achieving his M.Div. in 2009, he returned later for additional study in Christian psychology. Matt married his lovely wife Rachel in 2011, and together they have had several beautiful bio and foster children. In addition to his day job as a consulting software engineer, Matt has served as an elder at Franklin Street Church for several years.

If you would like to reach Matt, he is available by email at mattlewellyn3@gmail.com.

CPSIA information can be obtained
at www.ICGtesting.com
Printed in the USA
BVHW08051508062I
608943BV00014B/2758